B

Students Must Write

Students Must Write

A guide to better writing in course work and examinations

Robert Barrass

METHUEN
London and New York

First published in 1982 by
Methuen & Co. Ltd
11 New Fetter Lane, London EC4P 4EE

Published in the USA by
Methuen & Co.
in association with Methuen, Inc.
733 Third Avenue, New York, NY 10017

Typeset by Rowland Phototypesetting Ltd
Bury St Edmunds, Suffolk
Printed in Great Britain at the University Press, Cambridge

British Library Cataloguing in Publication Data

Barrass, Robert
Students must write.
1. English language – Writing – Study and teaching
I. Title
808'.042   PE1408

ISBN 0-416-33620-5

Library of Congress Cataloging in Publication Data

Barrass, Robert.
Students must write.

Bibliography: p.
Includes index.
1. English language – Style.   2. Authorship.
I. Title.
PE1421.B3   1982   808'.042   82-8237

ISBN 0-416-33620-5 (pbk.)

Contents

	Acknowledgements	viii
	Preface	ix
1	**Success at school and afterwards**	1
2	**Writing for yourself**	8
	Writing helps you to remember 8	
	Making notes during a lecture 8	
	Making notes during practical work 12	
	Capturing your thoughts 12	
	Writing helps you to observe 12	
	Writing helps you to think 13	
	Improve your writing 14	
3	**Writing to others**	16
	Writing letters 17	
	Improve your writing 25	
	Applying for employment 25	
4	**Essentials of clear writing**	30
	Conveying information 30	
	Illustrations contribute to clarity 32	
	Numbers contribute to precision 37	
	Reading critically 38	
	Improve your writing 40	

5 Writing and thinking   41
Think before you write   41
Select effective headings   42
Prepare a topic outline   42
Maintain order   43
Write at one sitting   46
Revise your work   47
Improve your writing   50

6 Thoughts into words   53
Vocabulary   54
The meaning of words   57
The words of your subject   62
Abbreviations   63
Improve your writing   64

7 Using words   67
Words in context   67
Superfluous words   69
Reasons for verbosity   73
Improve your writing   77

8 Helping your readers   80
Write for easy reading   81
How to begin   81
Control   81
Emphasis   83
Rhythm   85
Style   85
Capture and hold your reader's interest   86
How to make your writing interesting   87
Improve your writing   87

9 Finding information   93
What to read   94
How to read   98
Making notes as you read   98
Improve your writing   100

10 Writing an extended essay or a project report   102
Choosing a subject   102
Assessing extended essays and projects   103

Preparing an extended essay or project report   104
Arrangement   104
Writing   106
Improve your writing   108
*Checking an extended essay
or project report*   108
Presentation   109

11   Doing your best in examinations   111
Preparation   111
Why many students do not get
as many marks as they could   112
Technique   114
*How examination papers are
set and marked*   114
*Making the best use of your time
in an examination*   115
*Answering questions
in an examination*   116
Improve your writing   118

12   Speaking for yourself   120
Asking questions   120
Answering questions: being interviewed   120
Taking part in a tutorial   123
Preparing for a seminar   124
Giving a talk   124
Preparing and planning   125
Delivery   126
Visual aids   127
Using a blackboard   127
Using an overhead projector   128
Some tips on talking   128

Appendices   129
1 Punctuation   129
2 Spelling   135
3 The use of numbers in writing   141
4 Further reading   143

Index   145

Acknowledgements

I write not as a grammarian but as a teacher, knowing how important it is that students should be able to think clearly and to express their thoughts in writing.

For helpful criticisms and suggestions, I thank Richard Dimbleby, Head of Humanities at Somerset College of Arts and Technology, and Stewart Marshall, Senior Lecturer in the Department of Communication Studies, Sheffield City Polytechnic, who read the first draft; and John Dowling, Lecturer in English at New College, Durham, who read the typescript. I also thank my wife for her help, and Adrian Burrows for drawing the cartoons.

The comments of examiners, included in Chapters 1 and 11, are based on their reports on examinations taken by eighteen-year-old students in the UK. I am grateful to the Secretaries of different examining boards who provided reports on A Level examinations in all subjects.

The page from the *Notebooks* of Leonardo da Vinci (Fig. 1), from The Royal Library, Windsor, is reproduced by gracious permission of Her Majesty The Queen. The memorandum by Winston Churchill (in Chapter 7) is reproduced by permission of The Crown (CCR).

Preface

In all subjects at school and college, in applications for employment, and in all professions, the ability to express oneself clearly is an essential basis for success. Therefore, all students must write and all teachers should encourage their students to write well.

This book, by a teacher and writer, is a contribution to the teaching of English across the curriculum. It is for students of all subjects and for their teachers. It will be most useful to those in their last years at school and at college who, although they have been taught *English Language* for many years, still find that they need help in putting their thoughts into words.

This book can therefore be recommended by teachers of all subjects to all those students who would get better marks in course work and examinations if they could improve both their writing and their examination technique.

A section headed *Improve your writing* is included at the end of each chapter. This may be used by students who are working alone, or by teachers as a basis for course work in the use of English, non-specialist English, general studies or communication studies.

Robert Barrass
Sunderland Polytechnic

20 April 1982

1
Success at school and afterwards

Writing is important in all subjects at school and college, where you may write for several hours each day – in lectures, practical classes, seminars, tutorials and private study. You score marks for all written work, both indirectly if you can make good notes and directly if you can express your thoughts effectively in course work and examinations. In any subject, if students are equal in ability and intelligence, those who are able to convey their thoughts clearly in writing will get the better marks.

Students should consider the comments of examiners, to see if they can learn from them, otherwise only teachers and examiners will know how many marks are lost by candidates who give incomplete answers and include irrelevant material, and so do not show clearly whether or not they understand their work.

The following comments on the writing of eighteen-year-old students, who have been speaking English for seventeen years and studying English at school for thirteen years, are from the reports of examiners.

English Language and Literature

Some students wrote with charm and intelligence, displaying a love of books and of scholarship. Their work, written in clear, direct and simple English, was a delight to read. Others with limited practice in essay, précis, summary and comprehension techniques were easily identified. And there were also candidates who displayed in their writing a contempt for our language.

Most candidates should spend more time thinking about the meaning of the question and the words used, and should plan their work. They would then be able to write a considered answer. With such thought, the standard of answers would be raised.

English Law

Many candidates took no notice of the actual question set. Instead they wrote *all that they knew* about the subject and thus not only wasted valuable time but also demonstrated that they did not have a proper understanding of the subject.

Too many candidates fail to appreciate that a lawyer cannot function without a command of accurate punctuation and grammar. Bad English means bad law.

Engineering Science

Particular attention is drawn to the deplorable English of some candidates . . . poor sentence construction . . . lack of lucidity . . . dreadful spelling. This is a pity because in both higher education and industry great importance is attached to comprehension and communication skills.

History

The best scripts revealed an excellent knowledge and understanding of the topic discussed; and an ability to write an organized, fluent and cogent answer.

Time spent on teaching the art of writing is not time wasted. Even weaker candidates obtain higher marks after they have been properly taught to plan their answers and then to write concisely, intelligibly and in an orderly manner.

Everyone is capable of self-improvement. Good candidates can do better. Inevitably, clever candidates do not do as well as they should if they have not been properly trained in examination techniques.

Geography

The best candidates showed skill and perception when interpreting questions and writing appropriate answers. But some students with a great fund of knowledge do not achieve their full potential because they are unable to make intelligent use of their material. If they are to score high marks, students must learn how to answer the different types of questions they encounter in examinations and they must acquire sound skills in composition and in basic examination techniques.

Unfortunately, there are many candidates who fail to benefit from their knowledge of geography because mistakes in grammar and spelling render them incapable of expressing themselves unambiguously.

General Studies

Candidates should concentrate on reading and interpreting the questions, on planning organized answers, on relevance, and on writing clear and accurate English.

Even the most able eighteen-year-olds, who sit scholarship examinations, do not write as well as they should. The following comments are from an examiner's report on a scholarship paper in biology.

All answers included much irrelevant information.
Looseness of expression indicated lack of careful thought.
Very few answers were comprehensive.
Even when they knew the answer many candidates had difficulty in bringing facts together in an effective order.
Many candidates had the knowledge but were unable to express themselves.

The best English is to be expected from students of English Literature but, in a paper on critical appreciation, the examiners note:

Standards of punctuation and spelling, as well as of grammar, are still declining. Even quite good candidates spell words as though they have never seen them before, varying their spelling from one occasion to the next. This decline in literacy, now *very* marked, should be a matter of great concern.

If even clever school-leavers have difficulty with spelling, punctuation and grammar, and in selecting, arranging and expressing their thoughts, perhaps this indicates that there is something wrong with what is taught, and with how English is taught, in schools.

The purpose of all education *should be* to teach students to think; and to write well – so that they can express their thoughts effectively. Students should also be taught how to read; and to think about what they read – because reading, supported by personal observation and conversation, is the key to knowledge.

Dorothy L. Sayers, in *The Lost Tools of Learning* (1948) wrote:

> Modern education concentrates on teaching subjects, leaving the method of thinking, arguing and expressing one's conclusions to be picked up by the scholar as he goes along; . . . [Teachers] are doing for their pupils the work which the pupils themselves ought to do. For the sole true end of education is simply this: to teach men how to learn for themselves; and whatever instruction fails to do this is effort spent in vain.

Many students are clever enough to understand their work and yet unable to communicate their knowledge and ideas effectively. They need help with their writing more than further instruction in their chosen subjects.

Students are unlikely to appreciate that writing is so important in all subjects if the teacher of English is the only one who encourages them to improve their use of words. All teachers, therefore, should play their part in teaching the effective use of the English language.

> Being so long in the lowest form I gained an immense advantage over the cleverer boys. . . . We were considered such dunces that we could learn only English. . . . I learned it thoroughly. Thus I got into my bones the essential structure of the ordinary English sentence – which is a noble thing. . . . Naturally I am biased in favour of boys learning English. I would make them all learn English: and then I would let the clever ones learn Latin as an honour, and Greek as a treat.
>
> *My Early Life*, Winston Churchill (1930)

> English . . . includes and transcends all subjects. It is for English people the whole means of expression, the attainment of which makes them articulate and intelligible human beings, able to inherit the past, to possess the present and to confront the future. It is English in this sense that we must teach our children all day long, at all stages in their school life . . .
>
> *English for the English*, George Sampson (1925)

> If only teachers [of all subjects] would teach their pupils to think out every problem, and insist that all questions be answered thoughtfully and clearly, this salutary and indeed indispensable discipline and exercise of the mind would immensely improve the pupils' speech and writing, not merely in the English class but also in every other, not merely in school but outside.
>
> *English: a Course for Human Beings*, Eric Partridge (1949)

All your education depends upon the understanding and effective use of your language. Only by writing well can you give a good account of yourself (see table 1) as a student, or when you apply for employment, or as an employee – writing letters, instructions, reports, etc. If you intend to do well at school and in your chosen career, the ability to express your thoughts clearly in speaking and writing is a most important skill – and one that you should be trying to develop.

Table 1 *Judged by your writing*

Characteristics of your writing?	Impression created
writing clear	considerate
correct spelling	well-educated
punctuation and grammar good	competent
arguments well presented	forceful
writing illegible	inconsiderate
poor spelling	lazy
poor punctuation and grammar	careless or uneducated
arguments poorly presented	incompetent

Those who are unable to express themselves clearly when they leave school do not suddenly acquire this ability when they enter higher education. In an article in the *Times Higher Education Supplement* in 1976 Professor A. L. F. Rivet of the University of Keele wrote of the poor English of bright students whose teachers 'have neglected to instruct them in the elements of literary expression':

There is very little difference here between scientists and art students . . . after eleven years experience of marking foundation year essays, I am quite sure that the standard of written English is falling . . .

And, according to a report in the *Times Higher Education Supplement* in 1981, an inter-faculty committee of the University of Glasgow concluded that 25 per cent of first year students in arts, science, and social science needed help with basic writing skills.

In school, teachers of English set compositions and essays; and in all subjects at school and college you have to give written answers to questions – in course work, homework, and examinations. By showing how your writing could be improved, all your teachers at school and college should help you to do better work.

The power of rightly chosen words is great but there is no short cut to better writing. You can help yourself by noting the kinds of mistakes that most beginners make. Finding faults in the writing of others will help you to recognize your own mistakes and so to improve your own work. Some common faults in students' written work (see also p. 50) are as follows:

1 lack of planning;
2 failure to answer the question;
3 lack of balance;
4 failure to capture and hold the reader's interest;
5 the use of a long word when a short word would be better; and the use of more words than are needed to convey the intended meaning precisely; and
6 lack of care.

Improve your writing

1 Why do some students score higher marks than others in course work and examinations? Are they: (a) more intelligent; (b) harder working; (c) better organized; or (d) better able to communicate their thoughts?

   Intelligence, hard work and good organization are necessary if you are to do well. You must also be able to communicate your thoughts effectively in writing.

2 Work to a timetable throughout your studies. Include, in a pocket diary, the times when you have classes and the times for private study. Make use of free periods and evenings. Plan to complete some task in each study session. Set aside time for exercise, perhaps by walking or cycling to and from school or college. Set aside one evening each week, and some time at the weekend, for other kinds of relaxation. Get enough sleep.

3 To be good at any sport, or to play any musical instrument well, you must practise regularly. Similarly, to write well you must practise writing – but you can also learn by considering the advice of experienced and successful authors:

William Somerset Maugham. Write as simply as you can – as though you were writing a letter to a friend.

J. B. Priestley. Write as often as possible. Read good authors critically . . . noticing how they work.

Nicholas Monserrat. Never copy other writers. Never wait for inspiration. Get something down on paper . . . and look at it the next morning to see how you can improve it.

Evelyn Waugh. Success depends upon natural talent developed by hard work.

P. G. Wodehouse. The one essential is to have patience.

If you write badly it is probably because you have not thought sufficiently about what you wish to say. To write well, both at school or college and afterwards, think before you begin: whom do you expect to interest and what do you intend to tell them? Write of things that you know best and try to express your thoughts as clearly and simply as you can.

2

Writing for yourself

So much of what you write is intended for other people, enabling you to influence their thoughts and actions, that it is easy to overlook your other reasons for writing. You write as part of your day-to-day work: to help you to observe, to remember, and to think, as well as to communicate. Above all, writing helps you to think and to arrange and express your thoughts. Anyone who writes badly, therefore, is handicapped in private study as well as in dealing with other people.

Writing helps you to remember

At school, your first use of writing as an aid to remembering is in writing complete sentences dictated by your teachers. Later, especially in the last two years when you are learning to be a student, you make notes while you are reading (see p. 98), during your own investigations (in practical classes, field work or projects), and while your teacher is speaking.

Making notes during a lecture

You can make the most effective use of your time during a lecture if you have made some preparations. You should therefore look at the syllabus so that you have an idea of what is included in each year of the course. Remember that the syllabus is only a guide. You will need to attend every lecture to find out what the course comprises.

Lecturers should ensure that students can see either the syllabus or a summary of the syllabus for each year of their course. Each lecturer should provide, at the start of term, either a list of lecture titles with the date of each lecture or a list of topics to be considered each week. They should also provide a reading list, comprising details of important books that are available in the library and textbooks that each student is expected to buy. Without this information students cannot know what reading might be useful preparation for their next lecture.

Most lecturers write a title on the blackboard before they speak. Start by writing this title and the date at the top of a clean sheet of paper. During the lecture you should not need to write all the time. You should be listening carefully, thinking, and trying to understand. In speech we may use more words than are necessary in writing (see p. 74). Lecturers, especially, are likely to say something, and then rephrase what they have just said in an attempt to ensure that everyone understands. Then they may repeat things for emphasis; or summarize what they have said at the end of each part of their lecture to help you to recognize and record the most important points. In taking notes, therefore, it is neither necessary, nor desirable, to record every word.

Take your cue from the lecturer. Sometimes he (or she) will be trying to give you a complete set of notes, knowing that the information is not readily available from other sources: then he may state the most important points almost as in a dictation. Sometimes he will speak quickly all the time – leaving you to write carefully chosen headings for each new subject discussed, and sub-headings for each aspect of the subject (that is to say, for each topic).

Note the main points as key words and phrases. Use abbreviations. Record numbers, names, dates and titles. Write definitions carefully as they are dictated. Record the lecturer's conclusions clearly and concisely.

Mark any points that you do not understand, perhaps by a question mark in the left-hand margin. Then you will be ready to ask questions at the end. Note the answers to your questions and listen to other questions and answers, noting anything that contributes to your understanding.

Copy simple diagrams carefully while the lecturer is drawing. He should give you time to study any diagram, without the distracting effect of his voice.

The lecturer may start by saying how he is going to treat the subject. He may write the main headings on the blackboard; and will emphasize certain aspects or summarize the main points at the end. If the lecture has been well planned, your notes should contain a summary of the essential points – an orderly sequence of topic words and phrases (as numbered headings), with enough supporting detail (marked by letters: a, b, c etc.) – similar to the topic outline prepared by the lecturer (see p. 42) when he was deciding what to say.

Remember that the lecturer's task is not to provide you with a neat set of notes – by dictating a summary of your textbook – but to provide a digest of the essentials of the subject supported by examples; to discuss problems, hypotheses and evidence; to explain difficult points, concepts and principles; to refer to sources of information; and to answer questions. In this way the lecturer acts as a pacemaker. By listening, thinking and understanding, you are able to move forward more quickly than would be possible if you worked alone. However, you will find it easier to understand and to make useful notes during a lecture if you have done some preliminary reading (see table 2) and if you have understood the earlier lectures in the same course.

You should either listen to the lecture and then go to your books, or make notes as you follow the lecturer's explanations, arguments, and conclusions. Whichever method you adopt, you should learn throughout the lecture and should be ready to ask or answer questions at the end.

Note-taking helps you to remain attentive. Selecting the most important points to record helps you to learn to distinguish what is most important from the supporting details. See also: *Making notes as you read*, p. 98.

Good concise notes help you to remember the essentials of a subject. They can be read and reread, and you can add to them throughout your course of study as you get a firmer grasp of your subject. Good notes are an aid to all your studies and they are essential to revision before an examination, when you would not have time to read long and detailed notes.

Use wide-lined A4 paper (210 × 297 mm) for all your written work. Narrow-lined paper is not suitable either for your own notes or for course work because there is no space between the lines for minor additions or corrections. In making notes leave wide margins on both sides of the sheet and leave gaps for additions. It is also a good idea to write on one side of the page only. You will then have plenty of space for additions and corrections based on your observations in practical work, on your reading (see ch. 9), and on your own thoughts. Your aim should be to have one set of notes which ties together all aspects of your work (see fig. 6, p. 99). Used in this way, note-taking is an aid to concentration, to active study, and to learning.

Because they are so important, try to make good notes from the start of any course. Some students use a bound notebook in which they make notes of many different lectures; but this does mean that when they go home they spend time copying them out. Most students use loose-leaf, wide-lined, A4 paper, and keep a separate folder for each subject.

This method has the following advantages.

1 Notes on any topic can be kept together.
2 Pages can be added or removed easily.
3 The order of topics can be changed.
4 Other relevant work can be kept in the same folder as your notes on the subject.
5 It is normally necessary to carry only note-paper and writing materials. Notes on each subject can then be transferred to the appropriate subject folder, kept at home, each evening.
6 This system also has the advantage that you are less likely to lose all your notes – the results of one, two or three years' work.

Try to develop an effective note-taking technique so that you can make good notes during a lecture, seminar or tutorial. Then check your notes, as soon as possible, while the ideas and information are fresh in your mind. Check that they are legible. Make corrections and minor ad-

Note-taking helps you remain attentive.

Make good notes so that you need not waste time rewriting them.

ditions. However, do not get into the habit of copying out your notes. This is likely to be a waste of time; and in copying you may make mistakes. Furthermore, if you attend several lectures each day, you will never have enough time to copy all your notes. Your study time is best spent on regular study, and on improving your notes as you learn more about your subject (see p. 99).

Making notes during practical work

As in a lecture, first write the date and then a title – whether your practical work is indoors or outside. Keep a record of what you do and of how you do it, of any materials or equipment used, and of any observations made. If possible, your observations should be recorded on data sheets prepared in advance. Data sheets are tables in which each column has a heading that reminds you of the information required and so helps you to ensure that your records are complete.

Your practical notebook, like a diary, serves as a permanent record of what you did each day. But it is also the basis for any report of the whole work that you may need to prepare for other people.

Capturing your thoughts

As a student, it is a good idea to get into the habit of making a note of useful thoughts that come to mind. Keep a few sheets of notepaper folded in your pocket so that you can note, for example, a topic outline for an essay, an idea for an interesting first paragraph or for an effective conclusion. Otherwise, your fleeting thoughts may be lost.

In *Goodbye to All That* (1957) Robert Graves describes a conversation with Thomas Hardy:

> He had once been pruning a tree when an idea for a story suddenly entered his head. The best story he had ever conceived, and it came – complete with characters, setting, and even some of the dialogue. But not having pencil and paper with him, and wanting to finish his pruning before the weather broke, he took no notes. By the time he sat down at his table to recall the story, all was utterly gone. 'Always carry a pencil and paper', he said, . .

Writing helps you to observe

Preparing an accurate description, like making an accurate drawing, helps you to focus your attention on an object or event. When one point has been adequately covered in your description, look for something else to describe. This will help you to ensure that your description is complete.

Observation is clearly more important in some subjects than in others: but it is important in the arts as well as in the sciences and engineering. Description is the basis of journalism – the reporting of current events, and of history – the interpretation of records of past events. Similarly, observation is more important in some careers than in others.

However, a carefully prepared description of an object or event may be part of any study. When appropriate, your writing – the whole or part of any composition – may be *descriptive* (a description of people, objects, scenes, etc.) or it may be *narrative* (a description of an event or sequence of events in chronological order).

Writing helps you to think

We may think in words or picture situations in our imagination; and then we use words to capture our thoughts and feelings for later consideration. Writing therefore is a creative process. Here are some quotations, from the works of famous people, about the connection between writing and thinking.

> Hardly any original thoughts on mental or social subjects ever make their way among mankind, or assume their proper importance in the minds even of their inventors, until aptly selected words or phrases have, as it were, nailed them down and held them fast.
>
> *A System of Logic*, John Stuart Mill (1875)

> the toil of writing and reconsideration may help to clear and fix many things that remain a little uncertain in my thoughts because they have never been fully stated, and I want to discover any lurking inconsistencies and unsuspected gaps. And I have a story.
>
> *The Passionate Friends*, H. G. Wells (1913)

> When someone says 'I'm no good at English', what he or she really means is . . . 'I'm no good at thinking straight, I can't talk sense, I'm no good at being myself'.
>
> *English for Pleasure*, L. A. G. Strong (1951)

> an English course consisting only of grammar would be very barren, and command of language is best obtained by using it as a vehicle for disciplining and recording thought and stimulating imaginative thinking.
>
> *The Language of Mathematics*, F. W. Land (1975)

English is not like other school subjects: it is the condition of all academic life. The teaching of English is therefore the point at which all education must start.

Writing helps you to arrange your thoughts on any subject (see table 2) and to plan your work (see Chapter 5). Preparing an essay or project report makes you set down what you know and helps you to recognize gaps in your knowledge. This leads you to a deeper understanding of your work and is a stimulus to further study.

Table 2   *Making notes as an aid to thinking and learning*

Before the lecture	In the lecture	After the lecture
Preliminary reading	Start on a new page	Check your notes
	Write date and title	Further
	Listen carefully	reading
	Make legible notes	Bibliographic details
	1 Headings ←———	Page numbers
	key words ←———	Information and
	phrases ←———	ideas
	2 Definitions	Observations in
	3 Conclusions ←	practical work
Prepare	4 References	Notes in practical
questions ——→	Ask questions	notebook
	Listen to discussion	Think
	Make additions in	Learn
	gaps in your notes	Remember
	Understand	Store your notes in
	Learn	appropriate file

The preliminary reading will help you to understand the lecture better than would otherwise be possible, and to make better notes, as well as to prepare questions. The arrows in this table represent additions to your notes as a result of work done before and after the lecture.

Improve your writing

1 Your lecture notes are for your own use: they are not normally seen by your teacher. However, a teacher may state, at the start of a lecture, that the students' notes will be collected and marked at the end. The lecture is then a test of the students' ability to understand what is said, to recognize and note the most important points, and

to record sufficient supporting detail. The teacher can then help to clear up any misunderstandings; and advise those students who have not taken good notes.

2 A teacher may ask a class of students to study and then describe a familiar object, or to observe and then describe an everyday event. Differences between the descriptions prepared by different students will result from differences in their ability to observe, to remember what they have observed, and to find appropriate words to express their observations. Differences may also be due to bias – to the observer's preconceived ideas which stand in the way of accurate reporting. This exercise provides a basis for a class discussion on the importance of writing as an aid to observation; and on the reasons for differences between descriptions of the same object or event.

3 Suggestions on the use of writing as an aid to thinking are included at the end of Chapter 5 (p. 50).

4 The best way to improve your writing is to *consider carefully your teachers' comments on all your written work*. Similarly, teachers should base instruction in the art of writing on criticism of their students' own work.

3

Writing to others

At school and college you must be able to communicate *your knowledge* of each subject and demonstrate – to both teachers and examiners – *your ability to think*. After completing your education your ability to express yourself continues to be important. The further you are from manual work, and the larger the organization that you work for, the more you will need to convey your thoughts in written and spoken words. Writing is important in all kinds of employment. An engineer, for example, works with measuring instruments and a pocket calculator, but his effectiveness as an engineer depends as much on his ability to make other people understand what he is doing as it does on the quality of his other work.

In preparing any communication the most important things to consider are: what information must be included, why is this information required, and by whom. It is not enough to have a good idea or to do good work; you must also be able to make other people understand what you are doing, why you are doing it, and with what result.

Whatever your career, your value as an employee will depend not only upon your qualifications, experience and special interests but also upon your ability to communicate information and ideas to other people. You will need to communicate with the people you work for and, as you take on the responsibilities of leadership, you will need to pass on clear instructions to others.

'Tell them to send shorter messages'

Keep all communications short and to the point.

Writing letters

When you write to people you know, clearly their opinion of you is not entirely based on what and how you write. However, when you write to people whom you have never met they will judge you in the only way they can – by your writing. You should therefore take care over the content, layout and appearance of any letter to make sure that it makes a favourable impression on the recipient (see table 3).

The organization of all except the shortest letters can be improved, and their length reduced, if you make a few notes of the points you wish to emphasize and then number them in an effective order. Then, having decided what to say, convey your message simply, clearly, concisely and courteously. These are the essentials.

Try to put yourself in the place of the recipient as you read your letter before signing it. Consider your reader's point of view and his likely reaction. A good letter is one that creates a favourable impression and enables you to convey information pleasurably, or to obtain the action or information you require.

When you write a business letter, remember there is no special *business English*. The only rule is to avoid words and phrases that you would not use in other kinds of writing.

Table 3   *Different kinds of letter and their tone*

Purpose of letter	*Tone*
Request for details (of a course of study, an appointment, an item of equipment). *Invitation* to a speaker.	Clear, simple, direct and courteous.
Application for an appointment.	Clear, direct and factual. Confident but not aggressive.
Complaint	Clear and direct but not aggressive.
Reply (to an enquiry or complaint) giving information, instruction or explanation. Reply to all the points raised in the enquiry.	Clear, direct, informative, polite, helpful and sincere.
Acknowledgement (of an enquiry or application). Acknowledgement by postcard.	Simple and direct. Discreet.
Letter of thanks	Appreciative.

Table 4   *A formal business letter*

Addresses should not be punctuated. Words such as company (Co.) and Limited (Ltd) may be abbreviated. The date should be given in full, without punctuation. The position and address of the recipient must be written as on the envelope. The salutation should be Dear Sir, Dear Sirs or Dear Madam, and the complimentary close: Yours faithfully (or, in the US, Yours truly). Your signature should be legible. The supporting details, if they are more than a few lines, should be sent on a separate sheet which should have a title. This and any other enclosures must be listed after the name of the sender under the heading Enclosures.

                                                          Address of sender

                                                          Date
Position and
address of
recipient

Salutation,

                              Subject heading

          1   Information required

          2   Supporting details

          3   Conclusions and/or action required

              Complimentary close

              Signature

              Typed name and
              position of sender (if the letter is typed)

Enclosures: (List)

Reference line (if the letter is typed): initials of the person signing the letter and those of the typist.

Table 5   *An example of a formal business letter*

                                                            Your address

                                                            Date letter is signed

The Academic Registrar
Name of institution
and full address

Dear Sir,

    Could you please send further particulars of your course in
_____ _____ . I shall be taking my
_____ examinations, in two years time, in the following
subjects: _____ , _____ , and _____ .
    I should be grateful if you would also confirm that these do provide a
satisfactory basis for your course, or let me know of any special admission
requirements.

                              Yours faithfully,

Table 6 *A personal business letter*

This type of letter is used in business when the correspondents have met or when they know one another well from conversations on the telephone or from previous correspondence. The address should not be punctuated: no words should be abbreviated. The date should be given in full, without punctuation. The salutation includes the name of the recipient, and the complimentary close is normally Yours sincerely. Your signature should be legible. The name and address of the recipient, as written on the envelope, is in the bottom left hand corner of the letter.

                                                    Address of sender

                                                    Date

Salutation,

            1   Information required
            2   Supporting details
            3   Conclusion and/or action required
                Complimentary close

                Signature

                Typed name of sender

Name and address
of recipient

Enclosures: (List)

Reference line: sender's initials and those of the typist.

Table 7   *The use of a postcard*

A: *Correct use*

Date

Omit salutation

Message: note that a postcard may be seen by other people, as well as by the person addressed. When a postcard is used to acknowledge the receipt of a letter, therefore, the reply should not make public the contents or purpose of the letter: it should include only the date of the letter and, if there is one, a reference number.
Omit complimentary close.
The message should be followed immediately by the signature and the typed or printed name and address of the sender.

B: *An example*

Date card is signed

Thank you for your letter of ————————————————— which is
receiving attention.

Signature of sender

Position and
address
of sender

A reference line may be included,
as in a business letter.

Table 8 *Forms of address (to be used on the envelope)*

Mr John Smith (if John Smith is an adult)

Mrs John Smith (to John Smith's wife)[1]

John Smith Esq. (if you wish to indicate your respect)

Miss Jean Smith (if Jean Smith is unmarried)[2]

Master John Smith (if John Smith is a child)

John Smith (if John Smith is an adolescent)

Miss Jean Smith, BA PhD or Dr Jean Smith[2]

John Smith Esq., BSc PhD or Dr John Smith[3]

Messrs John Smith & Sons[4]

Notes

1 Some married women, especially if they are in business or the professions, prefer to use their maiden name.

2 In business correspondence a woman should indicate how she wishes to be addressed, for example by typing Miss Jean Smith, Dr Jean Smith or Mrs John Smith, immediately below her signature.

3 A man may type, below his signature, either John Smith or Dr John Smith, but he should not call himself Mr John Smith or John Smith Esq. When Esq. is used, in an address, no other title should stand before the name.

4 The prefix Messrs (F. *Messieurs*), as the plural of Mr, is now rarely used in business correspondence. Letters are usually addressed to an individual by name or to The Secretary or The Manager, etc. However, the term Messrs is acceptable in addressing firms with personal names, e.g. Messrs John Smith & Sons. It is not used in addressing limited companies or firms which do not trade under a surname.

For guidance on the correct use of titles and other distinguishing marks of honour or office, see *Titles and Forms of Address*, A. & C. Black, London.

Most letters are written on one page. In a few words you must pass on your message and create the right atmosphere between yourself and the person addressed. The tone of the letter will depend upon your purpose (see table 3) but no letter should be discourteous.

To keep each communication short and to the point, any necessary supporting details or further information should be referred to briefly but sent as an enclosure.

The initiator of any correspondence should state the purpose of the letter either by a clear, precise and specific heading, or in the first sentence. However, remember that the heading is not part of the letter and the purpose of the letter should always be made clear in the first sentence, which might begin: 'Please . . .', or 'I should be grateful if . . .'

The reply, and any further correspondence, should have an identical heading and should begin: 'Thank you for your letter of . . . about. . . .' From these beginnings both the writer and the recipient know immediately what each communication is about.

'Be ready to take a letter . . .'

In business a letter is usually a more satisfactory means of communication than a telephone conversation; and anything agreed on the telephone must be confirmed in writing.

Answer letters promptly unless there is some good reason for delaying your reply. A prompt reply makes for efficiency, enabling you to complete a task, and your courtesy impresses the recipient favourably. Letters have not been superseded by other means of communication. Anything agreed on the telephone must be confirmed in writing, normally on the same day. Misunderstandings are possible unless both parties have an accurate record of their conversation.

Every letter must fit into the filing system (records) of both the sender and the recipient. It should therefore deal with one subject only. If you have to write about more than one subject to the same person, each should be dealt with in a separate letter, even if these are enclosed in the same envelope.

Forms of address, to be used on the envelope, are suggested in table 8. Ensure that the address on the envelope is identical with that used in the letter, because you may need to check, later, from your copy of the letter, that the envelope was correctly addressed. If appropriate, you may wish to write *Personal* or *Confidential* in the top left-hand corner of the envelope.

Improve your writing

Applying for employment

Writing a letter is an exercise which most students will find useful and interesting. This is a good place to start teaching or learning the essentials of clear, concise and courteous writing.

Writing a letter is a test of your ability to communicate effectively – in appropriate language. Write a letter applying for a vacation job or for the kind of work that you would like to do after completing your education. Remember that the way a letter of application is written may be all that an employer needs to indicate that the applicant is not suitable for the job. Whenever you write a business letter, such as an application, take care over its appearance.

1 *Use unlined white paper* (size A4 = 210 × 297 mm).
2 Write legibly or type the letter.
3 Leave adequate margins.
4 Keep a rough copy or, if your letter is typed, keep a carbon copy.
5 Use a white envelope.
6 Fold the paper twice so that it fits neatly into the envelope.

The success of your application, in enabling you to obtain an interview (see p. 120), will depend not only on the care with which you prepare the application but also upon your interests and suitability as indicated in your application.

An application is normally in two parts: (1) a letter of application; and (2) a *curriculum vitae* (*c.v.*) on a separate sheet enclosed with your letter (see Tables 9 and 10).

In the letter you ask to be considered for this particular vacancy and you state why you are applying: for example, why you consider that you are suitable and why you think that you would find the work interesting.

In the *curriculum vitae*, state your name, date of birth, nationality, marital status, address and telephone number. Name your school. List the subjects you studied (or are studying) at school and give the results of any school examinations. Similarly, name your college, list the subjects you are studying and give the results of any examinations. List your hobbies, clubs, sports and other non-academic interests. Mention any weekend or vacation work or other work experience, especially if this is relevant to the work for which you are now applying. Give the names of two referees. One of these should be able to speak of your character and non-academic interests, and the other should be a teacher or someone you have worked for recently. Choose your referees carefully, *for each application*, to make sure they are appropriate, and remember to ask their permission before you give their names.

Include dates in your *curriculum vitae* (see table 10), so that it is a summary of all the important events and achievements in your life that are likely to interest *this employer*. Ensure that every year is properly accounted for: otherwise the employer may wonder if you have something to hide.

As in any other composition, consider your readers. If the post has been advertised some details will be given in the advertisement. You may then write for further details and an application form (which you should use instead of a *curriculum vitae*). The further details will tell you more about the post advertised and about the employer.

If you have to complete an application form, first read it carefully and prepare your answers to the questions on separate sheets. Copy them on to the form when you are satisfied that they are the best answers that you can give. Be careful to obey any instructions. For example, you may be asked to write in black ink or to answer certain questions in block capitals. You must answer all the questions, even if you write only *none* or *not applicable*.

It is best to make corrections and improvements on a first draft of your application until you are satisfied that you know how best to present yourself. Then, if there is time, put the draft on one side for a few days. Read it again and try to think how the recipient will react. Imagine that

Table 9   *An example of a letter of application*

Your address

Date letter is signed

The Personnel Officer
Name of firm
and full address

Dear Sir,
    Please consider this application for the post of _____
_____ (Ref. no. _____), advertised in _____
_____ on ____ _____ ___ .
    I am just completing an honours degree course in _____
_____ at _____ _____ . I was deputy head boy at school,
and have worked in a supermarket and in a factory. I have also travelled
in _____ . I enjoy working with other people and should like to
make a career in _____ _____ . I have a particular interest
in _____ _____ . A *curriculum vitae* is enclosed.
    I shall be taking my final examinations in _____ . Other-
wise, I could come for interview at any time convenient to you.

      Yours faithfully,

Table 10   *An example of a* curriculum vitae

Thomas Jones   Date of birth: 15 January 1980
British
Single
Home address:
Telephone no.

1991–8 _____ High School, _____ , _____
   1996 _____ examination results
      English   B   Science   C
      History   C   Mathematics B
      Geography A   French   A

   1998 _____ examination results
      English   A
      History   B   Further mathematics B
      Economics B

1998– _____ University
   Studied English, economics and mathematics.
   Reading for honours degree in economics.
   Final examinations in June 2001.
   Non-academic interests. At school I was deputy head boy and played
   rugby for the 1st XV. At university I play squash for the 2nd team. I
   enjoy reading, listening to music and going to the theatre. In the
   school holidays I worked in a supermarket. I travelled in
   _____ in the summer of 1999; and had a labouring job
   with _____   _____ for 8 weeks in the
   summer of 2000.

   Referees   _____   _____
             Personnel Manager   Senior Lecturer
            _____ _____   Department of Economics
            _____   _____ University
            _____

                          (Sign and date)   ....

the reader will be middle-aged, and that he or she is looking for someone with respect for authority, with a positive personality, who is likely to get along well with other people and accept responsibility. You may ask a friend to read your application.

Either have your application typed *or* write it again, legibly and neatly (see p. 118). Post it to arrive before the closing date. Keep a carbon copy, or your final draft, for future reference.

Making the most of yourself in an application is clearly a time-consuming job, but it is worth spending several hours on this work if you are trying to obtain suitable employment for a whole vacation or possibly for the rest of your working life.

4

Essentials of clear writing

The author of a novel or short story does not have to explain everything or make his meaning clear. He uses his imagination and leaves some things to the reader's imagination.

Imaginative writing will be encouraged in some literature and language essays, but your writing in course work and examinations in other subjects will be mainly factual. Your purpose will be to convey information clearly and concisely, and you will intend to leave nothing to your reader's imagination.

Conveying information

We all use instructions: how to use a piece of equipment; how to service a car; how to make bread, etc. Each set of instructions is a communication. Consider what you expect when you follow instructions.

1 *Explanation* The instructions should have a heading. As in a recipe, there should be a list of the materials required to complete the task. Then the writer should explain what you have to do.

2 *Clarity* The instructions should be clear so that they are easy to understand.

3 *Simplicity* You would expect the instructions to be as simple as possible.

4 *Completeness* If anything essential is omitted you would be unable, by following the instructions, to complete the task. The instructions, therefore, must be complete.

5 *Accuracy* You would expect the writer to have worked through the instructions to make sure that there were no mistakes.

6 *Order* You would expect things to be arranged in the right order: the order in which things are to be done. Each step should be distinct, and preferably it should be numbered, so that you know you have completed one step before you start the next.

The need for sufficient explanation, for clarity, simplicity, completeness and accuracy, and for the orderly presentation of information, is most obvious in preparing instructions, but they are essential in all except imaginative writing. Whatever you write, always prepare your work carefully.

1 Include sufficient *explanation*.
2 Make your meaning *clear* throughout.
3 Convey your message as *simply* as you can.
4 Make sure that your work is *complete*.
5 Check your work carefully, and make any corrections, to try to ensure that every statement is *accurate*.
6 Arrange the parts of your composition in an effective *order* – which best suits your purpose.

The writing of considerate authors, who wish to help their readers (and so help themselves to convey information pleasurably), has all these characteristics:

accuracy
appropriateness (to the subject, to the reader, and to the occasion)
balance (showing an awareness of all sides of a question; maintaining a sense of proportion)
clarity
completeness
consistency (in the use of numbers, names, abbreviations, spelling, punctuation, etc.)
control (paying careful attention to arrangement, presentation and timing – so as to affect the reader in a chosen way)
explanation
impartiality (unbiased by preconceived ideas)
interest (holding the reader's attention)
order
persuasiveness (convincing the reader by evidence and argument)
precision (exact definition supported, as appropriate, by counting or by accurate measurement)
relevance (including no irrelevant material)

simplicity
sincerity (the quality of frankness, honesty)
unity (the quality of wholeness, coherence)

Illustrations contribute to clarity

Drawings and diagrams attract attention. They are an aid to explanation and help you to present information quickly, clearly and concisely. They should complement your writing. Consider them as part of your composition – not as ornament or as additions to work that is otherwise complete. Effective illustrations enable you to use fewer words than would otherwise be needed. You should therefore plan your composition so that information is presented in the most appropriate ways: in words and pictures.

Each illustration should have a concise heading and should be numbered, so that it can be referred to in any part of your composition. Illustrations should not be added at the end, as if they were an afterthought, but should be in the most appropriate places. If possible, the reader should be able to see each illustration when it is discussed; and there must be at least one reference to the illustration in the text.

Drawings. Each line in a drawing should be an accurate record of an observation. Because of this, drawing is both an aid to observation (see p. 12) and a summary of observations (see fig. 1). If the proportions are to be correct the drawing must be to scale and the scale should be marked on the drawing in metric units.

In a drawing, as in a photograph, three-dimensional objects are represented in two dimensions. The drawing represents things as they are seen at one time from one place. A drawing, therefore, may help the reader or it may mislead him. For many purposes a diagram may be better.

Diagrams. Some diagrams are not drawn to scale. Each line is not intended as an accurate record: it is the diagram as a whole that provides a useful summary (see fig. 6, p. 99).

Plans and maps. If a diagram is drawn to scale, the scale should be marked on the diagram in metric units. Such a diagram (a plan or a map) conveys information more accurately than a photograph or drawing of the same subject.

Diagrams used for presenting data or statistics are also drawn to scale. A *graph* shows how one thing varies relative to changes in another. The thing that people can control, such as the time at which readings are taken, must be plotted in relation to the horizontal axis of the graph.

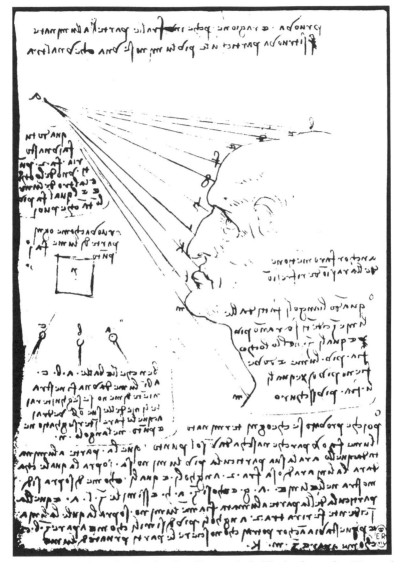

Fig. 1   *A page from the* Notebooks *of Leonardo da Vinci, who used writing and drawing as aids to observation and to the preparation of accurate records.*

To help the reader, when two or more graphs are to be compared they should be drawn to the same scale and, if possible, placed side by side.

The scales for the axes of a graph should normally start from zero; they should be chosen carefully and marked clearly. Units of measurement should be stated. All numbers should be upright but the labelling of the scales should be parallel to the axes (as in fig. 2).

Joining the points on a graph, by lines, may give a false impression; and to continue a line beyond the points drawn on a graph may mislead the writer as well as the reader. A remark by Winston Churchill, in another context, is appropriate: 'It is wise to look ahead but foolish to look further than you can see'.

Other kinds of diagrams, used for presenting numbers, are the *histogram* (fig. 3A), the *bar chart* (fig. 4A), and the *pictorial bar chart* (fig. 4B).

Percentages are effectively represented in a *pie chart* (fig. 5) in which 360° is equal to 100 per cent.

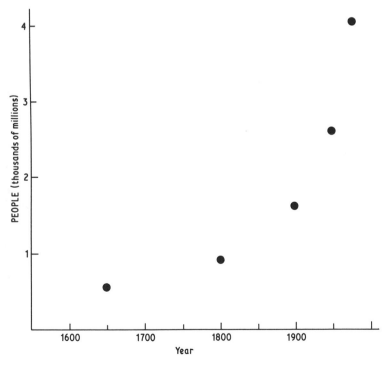

Fig. 2   *A graph: the growth of world population, 1650–1975*

The columns in a histrogram must be rectangles, not pictures, and they must be of equal width because it is the height of the column (not its width) that conveys information. If drawings are used (instead of columns) differences in area may confuse or mislead the reader (see fig. 3B).

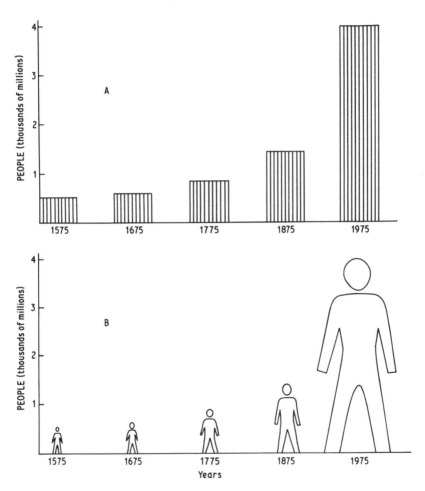

Fig. 3 A *A histogram, which may be used instead of a graph: the growth of world population, 1575–1975. B A pictogram – this is misleading because the symbols differ in width as well as in height. The area of a symbol does not accurately represent population size.*

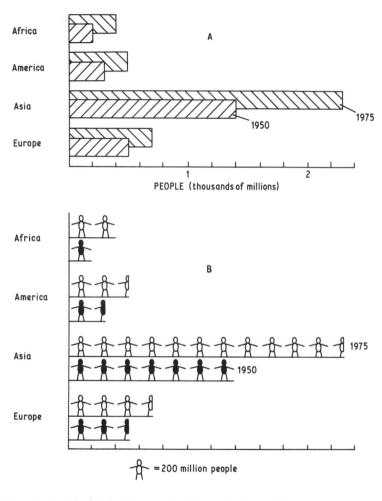

Fig. 4 A *A bar chart: the growth of the population in different world regions, 1950–75 (based on information presented in table 22, p. 82). Note that America includes Hawaii, Europe includes the USSR, and Oceania, which includes Australia and New Zealand and Pacific islands, is not included.* B *A pictorial bar chart which may be used instead of a bar chart.*

If symbols or different kinds of line or shading are included in any diagram, a key must be provided either on the diagram or in the legend.

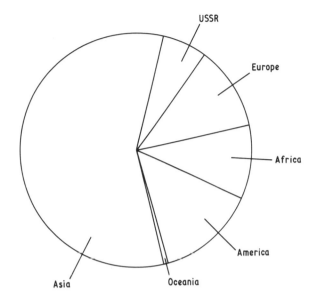

Fig. 5 *A pie chart: where people lived in 1975 (based on information presented in table 22, p. 82).*

Numbers contribute to precision

A politician may say that he firmly believes that a fund will be established 'of *substantial* size and *adequate* coverage over a *considerable* period'. He uses vague words to express his hopes when he is unable to be precise.

Consider the meaning that you wish to convey before you use the word *very* with an adverb (*very quickly*) or with an adjective (*very large*), and before you use other adjectives (such as *small, light, appreciable, large,* and *heavy*) or modifying and intensifying words (such as *actually, comparatively, exceptionally, extremely, fairly, quite, rather, really, relatively* and *unduly*). Vague statements will annoy the reader:

Whenever anyone says I can do something *soon* I'll say to them, yes, I know all about that . . ., but when, when, when?

Key to the Door, Alan Sillitoe (1969)

Be precise if you can: instead of *many, several* or *a few,* state how many.

Reading critically

Do not believe everything that you see in print, or take it for granted that the author's is the only possible point of view. Does the author tell you what you need to know? Criticizing the work of others should help you to recognize good writing and to improve your own written work. Each of the following extracts, from a book or magazine, is followed by a note of some faults.

Extract from a geography textbook

Much of the Romagna of Italy, for instance, which was fully populated in ancient times, was only restored to its ancient population and productivity by great efforts in the present century.

Some faults	
1 fully populated	This is imprecise. How many?
in ancient times	When?
2 only restored . . . by	This should read:
	restored . . . only by
3 to its ancient population	Very old people?
4 and productivity	As productive as in ancient times?

Extract from a book on examination technique

The complaints of examiners that students cannot write good English applies, I think, mainly to science students. Now science is founded on mathematics, and in general it is found that those who have an ability for literature are poor mathematicians and vice versa. . . . As their abilities lie outside literature, it is not surprising that science students write badly.

Some faults
1 The author should have written *either* that the complaints . . . apply, *or* that the complaint . . . applies.
2 The author is inconsistent. First he expresses an opinion and then states it as a fact.
3 The author makes the vague statement 'in general it is found that' but gives no evidence in support of this statement. In fact, some students of science write well and some students of literature write badly (see p. 3). Many people are good at both arts and science subjects. No students need feel discouraged: the more effort they put into any subject the more they will understand and enjoy it.

Extract from a magazine article by a Professor of education

The last ten years or so have seen changes in teaching of a magnitude unequalled in any previous period of our educational history. Such advances have necessitated a monumental expenditure of money and human resources, and it is interesting to note that whereas in countries like the United States . . .

Some faults
1 *Of a magnitude unequalled* means unequalled (see table 16, p. 61).
2 *In any previous period of our educational history* means in our educational history (see table 15, p. 60).
3 The *changes* mentioned in the first sentence are called *advances* in the second sentence.
4 *Advances* do not necessitate.
5 *Expenditure* cannot be monumental.
6 The words *it is interesting to note that* can be omitted without altering the meaning of the sentence (see table 11, p. 45)
7 Are any countries like the United States? The author means in some countries, including the United States, . . .

Extract from a learned journal

Safe and efficient driving is a matter of living up to the psychological laws of locomotion in a spatial field. The driver's field of safe travel and his minimum stopping zone must accord with the objective possibilities; and a ratio greater than unity must be maintained between them. This is the basic principle. High speed, slippery road, night driving, sharp curves, heavy traffic and the like are dangerous, when they are, because they lower the field zone ratio.

Some faults
1 The writer's meaning is not clear. Does he mean that a driver should always be able to stop within the distance that he can see to be clear?
2 The writer seems to have tried to make a simple subject unnecessarily complex.

Unclear, imprecise and unnecessarily complex writing is to be found in the most unexpected places: in textbooks, in learned journals, and even in the work of literary critics:

Many people write obscurely 'because they have never taken the trouble to learn to write clearly'. This sort of obscurity you find too often . . . even in literary critics. Here it is indeed strange. You would have thought that men who passed their lives in the study of the great masters of literature would be sufficiently sensitive to the beauty of language to write, if not beautifully, at least with perspicuity. Yet you will find in their works sentence after sentence that you must read twice in order to discover the sense. Often you can only guess at it, for the writers have evidently not said what they intended.

Another cause of obscurity is that the writer is himself not quite sure of his meaning. He has a vague impression of what he wants to say, but has not, either from lack of mental power or from laziness, exactly formulated it in his mind, and it is natural enough that he should not find a precise expression for a confused idea. This is due largely to the fact that many writers think, not before, but as they write.

The Summing Up, William Somerset Maugham (1938)

Improve your writing

Preparing a set of instructions is a good test of your ability to communicate effectively. Prepare instructions on how to replace the batteries in a portable radio; or how to complete some other simple task. Then try to perform the task, following your own instructions. If necessary, revise your instructions. Then ask someone else to perform the task, to see if they can follow your instructions or suggest any improvements.

5
Writing and thinking

Except in note-taking, when you write you are putting information and ideas together in your own way: you are composing. A letter to a friend; a written answer to a question in course work or examinations; a memorandum to a colleague in business, management, production or research; a report in a newspaper or a project report; an essay or an article in a magazine or journal: all these are compositions.

If you wish to improve your writing, you have taken the first step by recognizing the possibility of improvement. To ensure further improvement and so provide encouragement, you should treat every composition, however small, in the same way: *always think, plan, write and then revise*.

Think before you write

The first two stages – thinking and planning – will help you to get started and take you well on the way to completing your work. Planning may take a few minutes (as in an examination); or much more time may be spent on the search for information and ideas, and in discussion and thought. Irrespective of the time available, the first step is to organize your thoughts.

A good title should help you to define the purpose and scope of the composition, and it should inform the reader. Consider your readers. Who are they? Anticipate their questions. What do they need to know? How are you going to tell them?

Your readers want relevant information and ideas, well organized and clearly presented and with sufficient explanation. In conversation they would ask such questions as: Who? What? When? Where? Why? How? Ask yourself these questions. They serve as mental tin-openers. Your answers will lead to further questions. Consider the different areas of study, within your subject: are any aspects relevant to this composition? You will find that you know more about many topics than you at first supposed.

In a few moments of thought and reflection you will usually make a succession of relevant notes. You may use some of these as the topics for separate paragraphs and others as supporting ideas within a paragraph. You may leave out other points, in your selection of material, either because they provide unnecessary detail or because you choose better examples to support your argument.

Select effective headings

Look at the question and select appropriate headings to help you to identify all parts of the question, to ensure that you answer all parts of the question, and to ensure that these parts are answered in a logical order (which will normally be the order in which they appear in the question).

Headings are essential in helping you to think about your answer. They help you to check that everything included is relevant, not only to the question as a whole but also to the preceding heading. This helps you to avoid repetition and to get things into an effective order. Good headings and sub-headings also provide signposts for the reader (see also examination technique, p. 117). They are essential in a long composition, but some teachers may advise you not to use them in a short composition – such as an essay written in an examination. Also, what is encouraged in some subjects may be discouraged in others.

Prepare a topic outline

Consider the purpose and scope of your composition. As information and ideas come to mind, spread key words, phrases and sentences over a whole page, leaving plenty of space for additions. Use the main points as headings and note supporting details below the relevant heading. Then number the headings as you make the following decisions.

1 How is the subject to be introduced? Normally there should be a short, crisp introduction.
2 What is the topic for each paragraph?

3 What information and ideas must be included in each paragraph?
4 What should be left out? Cross out these points.
5 What needs most emphasis? Underline these points.
6 Are any simple diagrams needed and where should they be placed in your composition?
7 How can the paragraphs be best arranged in a logical sequence?
8 How can the composition be concluded effectively? Normally the last paragraph should be short and to the point. From thoughts presented in the preceding paragraphs you should come to an effective conclusion (see p. 46).

If you are writing a letter to a friend or a report for an employer, you will try not to include things that you expect the reader to know already. However, in course work or examinations you cannot omit definitions or important details, or leave things out because they seem obvious or because the reader knows them already. Every question set is a test of *what you know*, and of your ability to *select* what is relevant and to present this as an *organized* answer: it is a test of your ability *to think*. Your topic outline contributes to order and to the organization which is essential to writing. It will help you to deal with each aspect fully in one place, to avoid digression, and to maintain the momentum which makes a composition hold together.

If possible, put your topic outline on one side for a while. This may give you time to find additional information or to clarify your ideas; and it will enable you to have second thoughts. It is easier to add new topics to a list or to change the numbering of topics than to change your mind after you have started to write.

Working from your topic outline, you can write with the whole composition in mind. Each word should then contribute to the sentence, each sentence to the paragraph, and each paragraph to the composition. Only by working to a plan can you maintain control, so that you present your subject simply, effectively and without repetition.

Your topic outline will be particularly useful if, because of interruption or the pressure of other work, you are unable to complete your composition at one sitting.

Maintain order

Each composition may be compared to an old-fashioned railway train, with an engine, a number of carriages, and a guard's van. In a composition such as an essay, the first paragraph (the introduction) and the last paragraph (the conclusion) serve different purposes, resulting from their positions at the beginning and the end (like the engine and the guard's van). Each of the other paragraphs (like the carriages of a train) is a distinct and essential part of the whole but it also links what has gone before with what is to follow.

After the title and the introductory paragraph, further paragraphs should be arranged so that they lead logically to the closing paragraph. The logical order may be, for example, chronological or geographical. In a short work it may be an order of increasing importance, or in a long work an order of decreasing importance.

The first paragraph is your readers' first taste of what is to come. Here you must capture their interest. Your first paragraph must leave no doubt about the purpose and scope of the composition, but there are many ways of beginning (see p. 81).

There should be one paragraph for each aspect of the subject (for each topic) so that, as far as possible, you can deal completely with each topic in one place. Each paragraph should therefore be well ordered and clearly relevant, with a limited and well-defined purpose.

The topic for each paragraph is usually clearly stated (or is apparent) in the first sentence; but in an explanation or argument the topic sentence may come last. All sentences in the paragraph should show your understanding of the topic. They may provide *relevant* information, evidence, an example or ideas, and the first and last sentences should also help to link the paragraphs so that readers can see clearly how one paragraph leads logically to the next.

Because the first and last words in a paragraph attract most attention, never begin a paragraph with unimportant words. Omit superfluous phrases such as: *First let us consider.* . . . *Secondly it must be said that.* . . . *An interesting example which should be mentioned in this context is.* . . . *Next it must be noted that.* . . . *We can sum up then by saying.* . . . These thoughts should be going through your mind as you prepare your topic outline. They are an aid to thinking. How shall I begin? What shall I say next? Then what? How shall I conclude? Such questions help you but they are not for your readers (who require only the results of your thought).

Superfluous introductory and connecting phrases (see tables 11 and 12) distract the reader's attention. The change from one topic to the next should be signposted by a clear break between the paragraphs; and the new topic should be introduced directly and forcefully in the first words of each new paragraph.

Within the paragraph, each sentence should convey one thought. Punctuation marks should be used when they are needed to clarify meaning or to make for easy reading. Each sentence should be obviously

Table 11   *Introductory and connecting phrases which can usually be deleted without altering the meaning of the sentence*

It is considered, in this connection, that . . .
From this point of view, it is relevant to mention that . . .
In regard to . . ., when we consider . . ., it is apparent that . . .
As far as . . . is concerned, it may be noted that . . .
It is of interest to note that . . . of course . . .
From this information it is clear that . . .
It has been established that, essentially, . . . in the case of . . .
in the field of . . . for your information . . . in actual fact . . . with reference to . . .
in the last analysis

Table 12   *Introductory phrases which should usually be deleted*

Introductory phrases	A possible interpretation
arguably	I do not wish to commit myself
as is well known	I think
it is evident that	I think
it is perhaps true to say	I do not know what to think
it is generally agreed that	some people think
all reasonable men think	I believe
for obvious reasons	I have no evidence
there is no doubt that	I am convinced
to be honest	I do not always tell the truth
as you know	this is superfluous
as mentioned earlier	this is superfluous
it is not necessary to stress the fact	I should not need to tell you
with respect	I think you are talking nonsense

related to the preceding sentence and to the next. No new statement should be introduced abruptly and without warning. The sentences within each paragraph should therefore be in a logical and effective order so that they hold together and convey your meaning precisely.

Balance is important in writing, as in most things. The sentences in a paragraph and the paragraphs in an essay, like the handle and the blade of a knife, must be balanced in themselves and in relation to one another.

Your composition as a whole must be well balanced: ideas of comparable importance must be given similar emphasis.

Paragraphing breaks up the page of writing, provides a pause at appropriate points in your composition, and helps the reader to know that it is time to pass from one topic to the next. Short paragraphs are the easiest to read and so they make for efficient communication. However, paragraphs are units of thought, each with one thought or with several closely connected thoughts, and they will therefore vary in length.

Only you can decide if your composition is so long that the reader needs a summary; but a short composition prepared in an examination or in course work should not normally end with a summary. You should be able to make better use of your final paragraph: it is your last chance to affect the reader in a chosen way. The topics covered in your preceding paragraphs should have led to your conclusion; or they should have provided a basis for speculation; or they should allow you to emphasize some aspect of the subject which serves to link all paragraphs. Whatever method you adopt for bringing your composition to a close, the end should be obvious to the reader. It should not be necessary to begin the closing paragraph, as so many inexperienced writers do, with the words: 'In conclusion . . .'.

> The writer I like has paragraphs varied in length, development and organization. He . . . moves quickly through simple material, and explains . . . difficult points. His paragraphs are carefully connected, and when there is a marked change in thought, there are enough indications to help me to follow the shift. He does not repeat unnecessarily or digress; instead he covers his subject thoroughly and briefly. While I am still interested, he completes his work in a satisfactory final paragraph . . .
>
> *Effective Writing*, H. J. Tichy (1966)

Write at one sitting

Many professional people write in a busy office or in places where they are constantly interrupted by enquiries from colleagues, by telephone conversations, and by other tasks. Similarly, as a student you get used to working in a library where there may be some distractions. Perhaps you read each day on a train to and from college, or work on a topic outline when you have a few moments between other tasks. However, if possible, when you have finished thinking and planning, and are ready to write, it is best to put other work on one side and to write where you will be free from interruptions or distractions.

With your topic outline complete, the theme chosen, and the end in sight, try to write your composition at one sitting. Use the words that first come to mind. Stopping for conversation, or to revise sentences already written, or to check the spelling of a word, or to search for a better word, may interrupt the flow of ideas and so destroy the spontaneity which gives freshness, interest and unity to your writing. The time for revision is when the first draft is complete.

Work from your topic outline. Present information in a logical, interesting and straightforward way. Use enough words to make your meaning clear. Too few words will provide insufficient explanation and too many may obscure meaning and will waste the reader's time.

Arguments in favour of any idea expressed should be based on the evidence summarized in your composition. Where appropriate your statements should be supported by examples, so that the reader can judge their validity. Criticism of other people's work should be reasoned and not based on preconceived ideas for which you are able to present no evidence.

Revise your work

Two processes are involved in written communication. The first, in your mind, is the selection of words to express your thoughts. The second, in the mind of the reader, is the conversion of the written words into thoughts. The essential difficulty is in trying to ensure that the thoughts created in the mind of the reader are the same thoughts that were in your mind.

Too often, the reader is faced with an ambiguous sentence or a statement that is obviously incorrect and has to try to work out what the writer meant (see table 12, p. 45). You will need to revise carefully to try to ensure that your words do record your thoughts. Try to ensure that the reader takes this same meaning.

A common failing in writing is to include things in one place which should be in another. Indeed, one of the most difficult tasks is to get everything into the most effective order. One reason for this, even after careful planning, is that we remember things as we write. Information and ideas may then be included in one paragraph although they would be better placed in another.

In writing, we use words as they come to mind, but our first thoughts are not necessarily our best thoughts – and they may not be arranged in the most effective order. Wrong words and words out of place lead to ambiguity and distract the reader's attention, and so have less impact than would the right words in the right place. And inappropriate words, which are not suited to the reader or to the occasion, are barriers to easy communication.

By further thought, a writer should be able to improve a first draft.

If possible, put your composition on one side for at least a day and then revise it carefully so that readers do not have to waste time on an uncorrected first draft which may reflect neither your intentions nor your ability. Read the whole composition aloud to ensure that it sounds well and that you have not written words or clumsy expressions that you would not use in speech.

Thinking, planning, writing and revising are not separate processes, because writing is an aid to thinking. The time taken in planning, writing and revising is time for thought. It is time well spent, for when the work is complete your understanding of the subject will have been improved.

To admit that you need to plan your work and that you can improve your first draft is not to say that you are unintelligent. The apparent spontaneity of easy-reading prose is the result of hard work. Intelligence and effort are needed if a subject is to be presented as simply as possible. Simplicity in writing, as in a mathematical proof, is the outward sign of clarity of thought.

Every writer needs to correct and improve the first attempt. Flaubert (1821–80) had high self-imposed standards. He worked for hours at each page: writing, rewriting, reading aloud and recasting, trying to achieve balance and perfection. Colette (1873–1954) wrote everything over and over again and would often spend a whole morning working on one page. Maugham (1874–1965) said that if he achieved the effect of ease in his writing, it was only by strenuous effort. H. G. Wells (1866–1946) would write a first draft that was full of gaps, and then make changes between the lines and in the margin. Aldous Huxley (1894–1963) said 'All my thoughts are second thoughts'.

Those who write best probably spend the most time criticizing and revising their prose, making it clear and concise but not stultified – and ensuring a logical flow of ideas. However, revision must not be taken so far that the natural flow of words is lost. Alan Sillitoe said of *Saturday Night and Sunday Morning*: 'It had been turned down by several publishers but I had written it eight times, polished it, and could only spoil it by touching it again.'

In your work at school or college, you do not want to get into the habit of writing things more than once. Occasionally, you may rewrite an important essay or project report. However, even in examinations you should allow time to read through your answers – to make good any important omissions and to correct any obvious mistakes.

The pleasure to be derived from writing comes from the effort of creative activity – which should help you to learn about a subject and lead you to a deeper understanding. Each composition is original: it is a vehicle for self-expression, and involves you in organizing your thoughts and then presenting information and ideas *in your own way*. No one else would select the same material for inclusion, arrange the arguments in the same way, make the same criticisms or reach the same conclusions.

Pleasure comes from writing something that will affect other people. The reader may be persuaded or convinced by evidence logically presented, or may be annoyed or misled by poor writing. Each communication is a challenge to you to present information and ideas directly and forcefully, to help the reader along, *and to affect the reader in a chosen way* – for this is the purpose of all exposition.

Table 13   *How to write*

Think	1 Consider the title.
	2 Define the purpose and scope of your composition.
	3 Consider the time available and allocate your time to thinking, planning, writing . . .
	4 Decide who your readers are and what they need to know.
	5 Make notes of *relevant* information and ideas.
Plan	6 Prepare a topic outline.
	7 Underline the points which require most emphasis.
	8 Decide upon an effective beginning.
	9 Number the topics in a logical *order*.
	10 Decide upon an effective ending.
Write	11 Write on wide-lined A4 paper with a 25 mm margin – to leave yourself enough space for additions or corrections.
	12 See that you are free from interruption.
	13 Use the topic outline as your guide.
	14 Start writing, keep to the point, and keep going until your composition is complete – expressing your thoughts as *clearly* and *simply* as you can.
Revise	15 Leave yourself time to read through your work to make sure that every word is legible, that everything is relevant, and that nothing is repeated unintentionally; and to make any corrections or other improvements; and to check that all the points that you wished to emphasize are clearly made.
	16 Date all your work.

Improve your writing

The word essay means an attempt. It comes from the French verb *essayer*, to try. In an essay, you attempt to interest the reader; you attempt to create an original composition that is complete in itself. Preparing and writing an essay helps you to recognize your strengths and gives you the opportunity to make good any weaknesses. You will find that you learn about the subject at each stage in your preparation of an essay: from gathering information and ideas, from selecting and arranging your material, from writing and from revising.

1 When you have to write an essay choose a subject that interests you and which you already know something about, or read about the subject before you start to write – so that you can select, arrange and maintain control.

2 Write a topic outline for an essay, on a subject which is of particular interest to you. Your plan should comprise key words and phrases, the topics for paragraphs, and brief notes on each topic to remind you of information and ideas to be included in each paragraph. Use one page for rough work and then arrange your plan neatly on the next facing page.

3 When you are set work, you are given a date by which the work must be completed. Copy the question carefully and start work on your topic outline as soon as possible – to give yourself time for thinking, planning and writing, and for second thoughts.

   Teachers of all subjects can help their students by asking for a topic outline to be handed in with each essay. Students should then learn from their teachers' corrections and suggestions, and should ask about anything that they do not understand or that they wish to discuss.

4 To give students practise in preparing and writing an essay in about thirty minutes (as they will have to do in an examination), teachers may set a question and ask for both a topic outline and an answer to be completed quickly as a class exercise.

5 Reading an essay to other students, as a small group in a tutorial, can provide a basis for discussion. Considering ideas on presentation, or topics for paragraphs, or points of detail, may help all members of the group: they may learn more about their subject and about the art of communication. Consider the following common faults in students' written work.

Lack of planning. Information and ideas are presented in an ineffective order, or the logical order of the paragraphs is not apparent to the reader.

Lack of planning is also indicated when information on one topic, which should be brought together in one paragraph, is included in different parts of the composition. This confuses the reader and makes marking more difficult.

Failure to answer the question. Some students answer the question that they would have liked, instead of the question asked. This results from lack of attention to the precise wording of the question, from lack of understanding, or from wishful thinking.

Lack of balance. Too much attention is paid to some aspects, too little to others, and some are even ignored. Such unbalanced or incomplete answers may be due to lack of planning rather than lack of knowledge.

Teachers and examiners, to be fair to all students, use a marking scheme in which a fixed number of marks is allocated to each aspect of an answer. In course work and examinations you try to score marks. If you spend too much time on one aspect of an answer, you cannot score more than the number of marks allocated for this part. You are likely to get fewer marks for other aspects which you neglect. And you can score no marks for aspects which you ignore.

Failure to capture and hold the reader's interest. This fault also indicates a lack of planning. A student who wishes to interest his teacher must provide more than a summary of the teacher's own lecture. At least, he must select only relevant aspects of the lecture in answer to any question, and must present them in a logical order. If possible he should provide further evidence of his own thinking – by displaying knowledge gained from different lectures, from background reading or from personal observations, as appropriate. (See also Chapter 8.)

The use of a long word when a short word would serve the writer's purpose better and *the use of more words than are needed to convey the intended meaning precisely.* These faults may result from pomposity or from trying to make a little knowledge go a long way – perhaps in the belief that marks are given for the number of words used or the number of pages filled.

Lack of care. Many mistakes result from the student's failure to read through the composition. As a result, some sentences do not make sense, other sentences are ambiguous, and slips of the pen go uncorrected.

6 Criticizing compositions by other students will help you to improve your own. You will find it helpful, therefore, to look carefully at the written work of your friends – both before and after it has been marked. Similarly, you may benefit from their comments on your work. Can they understand every word and every sentence? Are they convinced by the evidence and by your arguments? Can they suggest improvements?

7 Learn to check your own work. In course work and examinations, you are usually trying to *explain* something *clearly* and *simply*. Remember that marks are given for *balance* (paying sufficient attention to each part of the question), for *accuracy* and *completeness*, and for the *orderly* presentation of *relevant* information and ideas.

8 Learn to improve your writing by studying the technique of successful essayists. Consider, for example, the purpose and scope of a leading article in a good newspaper, and of an article in a magazine. Study each article carefully.

Does the title of the article capture your interest?

Does the opening sentence make you want to read the article?

Reconstruct the writer's topic outline by picking out the topic for each paragraph.

Is each paragraph relevant to the title?

Are the paragraphs in a logical order?

Do they lead smoothly to an effective conclusion?

Are the arguments convincing?

Is the article biased?

Are all your questions answered?

6

Thoughts into words

Word games, such as *Scrabble* and crossword puzzles, are popular because there is fun to be had from words. Our pleasure and interest in words is not surprising, because when we speak or write we are trying to put our own thoughts into words. Indeed, the use of words is even more fundamental. Without words we cannot think; and we are limited in our ability to think by the number of words at our command. If we have a large vocabulary, and can construct effective sentences and paragraphs, we are better able to think and to express our feelings.

The habit of consulting a good dictionary (see p. 143) whenever you come across a word that you do not understand can be a lifelong source of enlightenment and pleasure. A dictionary provides excellent reading. As Eric Partridge (1949) pointed out in his *English: a course for human beings*, the stories in a dictionary are short but when you have read one you have learnt something:

. . . you understand the word the next time you see it in print or hear it spoken – and you can use it . . . without your companions glancing at one another in that odd way which is so much more disconcerting than outright laughter.

We write so that we can tell others what we think, but if we use words incorrectly, or use words that our readers do not understand, we shall be misunderstood. We must think about words so that we can use them correctly and so that we can choose words that we expect our readers to know.

Vocabulary

English is used for international communication, and people who read English as a second language are most likely to understand plain words in simply constructed sentences. Anyone who wished to be widely understood, therefore, would express his thoughts in simple language. One of the delights of English is its rich vocabulary. No two words have quite the same meaning, and the choice of one word when some other word makes more sense will not help the reader. When *The Times* newspaper reported that Rudyard Kipling was to be paid £1 a word for an article, a student sent £1 and asked 'Please send us one of your best words'. Kipling replied, 'Thanks'.

The right word is not always the first to come to mind, and people who have too few words at their command may fall back upon hackneyed phrases or clichés such as: *it goes without saying; at the psychological moment; in well-informed circles; feel compelled to admit; strange as it may seem; to all intents and purposes; with no shadow of doubt; in any shape or form;* and, *last but not least, conspicuous by his absence.* Instead, they should take trouble to find the word or words which express their meaning precisely.

'My dear, a rich vocabulary is the true hallmark of every intellectual person. Here now' – she burrowed into the mess on her bedside table and brought forth another pad and pencil – 'every time I say a word, or you hear a word, that you don't understand, write it down and I'll tell you what it means. Then you memorize it and soon you'll have a decent vocabulary. Oh, the adventure', she cried ecstatically, 'of moulding a little new life!' She made another sweeping gesture that somehow went wrong because she knocked over the coffee-pot and I immediately wrote down six new words which Auntie Mame said to scratch out and forget about.

Auntie Mame, Patrick Dennis (1955)

You may use words that you understand, and that your readers understand, yet still write sentences that are difficult to read. Try not to fill your writing with words that have been made longer by having bits added (for example; prove, approve, disapprove, disapproving; nation, national, nationalize, nationalization, denationalization). This is not to say that long words should never be used; but remember that long involved sentences with many long words make for hard reading.

Never use long words simply for effect. Prefer a short word to a long one (see table 14) unless the long word is more suitable; and prefer a single word to a phrase (see table 20) if brevity makes for clarity.

In *David Copperfield*, by Charles Dickens (1850), Mr Micawber had the habit of using long words to impress and then providing a translation so that he could be understood:

'Under the impression,' said Mr Micawber, 'that your peregrinations in this metropolis have not as yet been extensive, and that you might have some difficulty in penetrating the arcana of the Modern Babylon in the direction of the City Road – in short,' said Mr Micawber, in another burst of confidence, 'that you might lose yourself . . .'

Table 14   *Prefer a short word to a long word if the short word is more appropriate*

Prefer this . . .	to this
yes	absolutely
do	accomplish
extra	additional
expect	anticipate
use	application
help	assistance
begin	commence
about	concerning
so	consequently
much	considerable
show	demonstrate
give	donate
meet	encounter
except	excepting
build	fabricate
first	firstly
send	forward
guidance	guidelines
suggest	hypothesize
reputation	image
important	importantly
sign	indication
person	individual
people	individuals
please	kindly
methods	methodology
change	modification
partly	partially
people	personnel
nearly	practically

Table 14   *Continued*

Prefer this . . .	to this
go	proceed
preventive	preventative
about	regarding
is	represents
show	reveal
simple	simplistic
shortened	streamlined
later	subsequently
enough	sufficient
end	terminate
happen	transpire
use	utilize
almost	virtually

Some people like fashionable words, such as chairperson, deprived, dialogue, disadvantaged, escalation, hopefully, importantly, integrated, meaningful, nice, non-event, obscene, ongoing, overall, paradigm, relevant, situation, supportive, teach-in, traumatic and workshop. The rapid dating of such fashionable words is particularly clear in euphemisms for *poor* people. They became *needy*, then *deprived*, then *disadvantaged*, and then *underprivileged* – yet remained poor.

Fashionable words may lose their impact, because they are overused. They may be devalued, if they are used even when another word would be more appropriate. Discerning writers may then avoid such words, with the result that they may be words to avoid even after they have gone out of fashion.

When people thing that something is too technical for them, it may be that the writing is at fault. Unfortunately, some writers seem to think that scholarly writing must be hard reading, and that they impress people by adopting a pompous style. But their studied avoidance of short words is not likely to impress, and is very likely to annoy, confuse or amuse. This anonymous nursery rhyme pokes fun at grandiloquence.

> Scintillate, scintillate, globule aurific,
> Fain would I fathom thy nature specific,
> Loftily poised in the ether capacious,
> Strongly resembling a gem carbonaceous.

You know the rhyme? Perhaps you have heard something like it.

The meaning of words

As a guide to the meaning of words, to their origins, and to spelling, there should be a good dictionary on your bookshelf (see p. 143).

The habit of writing a word in inverted commas to indicate that it is not quite the right word, or that you are not using it in the usual sense, or that more is implied than is said, is likely to confuse people. Instead, choose the word or words which convey your meaning precisely.

Many people confuse the following: accept (receive) with except (not including); advice (counsel) with advise (to give advice); advise, with inform (to tell); amount (for mass or volume) with number (of things counted); affect (to influence) with effect (to cause *or* a result); complement (to make complete) with compliment (to congratulate); defective (not working properly) with deficient (without some essential); dependant (one who is dependent) with dependent (relying upon); deprecate (disapprove) with depreciate (decrease in value); enquiry (a question) with inquiry (an investigation); farther (more distant) with further (additional); fewer (in number) with less (in quantity); forego (go before) with forgo (go without); fortunate (lucky or prosperous) with fortuitous (accidental); its (possessive) with it's (it is); a licence (a permit) with to license (to grant a permit); majority (the greater number or part) with most (nearly all); of course (certainly) with off course (not on course); each other (which refers to two) with one another (referring to more than two); practical (not theoretical) with practicable (feasible); a practice (a noun) with to practise (a verb); principle (a truth) with principal (main); stationary (not moving) with stationery (writing paper); to (as in to go) with too (as in too much); true (real) with valid (sound); uninterested (not interested) with disinterested (impartial); venal (person who may be bought) with venial (pardonable); verbal (using words) with oral (spoken).

Approximate (ly) means very close (ly) and should not be used when *about* or *roughly* would do better.

Data (L. *dare*, to give) refers to things given or observations (facts of any kind) and should not be confused with *results* (which are obtained by the analysis of data).

Infer does not mean the same as *imply*. The writer or speaker implies something but the reader or listener infers.

Initiate means begin something; to *instigate* is to persuade someone else to do something.

Often: 'People who eat mushrooms often die.' (But people who do not eat them die only once?)

Refute should be used in the sense of proving falsity or error. It is not a synonym for deny or repudiate.

While means at the same time as: 'Nero fiddled while Rome burned.' Do not write while if you mean *and* or *but*: 'I prefer squash while you prefer tennis'; 'On Saturday I work while on Sunday I rest'.

Write *consists of* or *comprise* (not comprise of); write *different from* (not different to); and write *superior to* (not superior than).

Certain other words and the prepositions that should follow them, according to accepted usage, are the following: absolve from, abstain from, accompanied by, in accordance with, amenable to, collaborate with, compatible with, confirm in, conform to, connive at, consequent upon, correspond to (a thing), correspond with (a person), concur in (an opinion), concur with (a person), defer to, deficient in, impervious to, indifferent to, indicative of, independent of, irrespective of, ineligible for, militate against, oblivious of, preferable to, preoccupied with, refrain from, responsible for (an action), responsible to (a person), substitute for, but replace by.

Many people misuse the following words: access (for excess); aggravate (for annoy); alibi (for excuse); allude (for refer); alternatively (for alternately); alternative (for choice); always (for everywhere); appreciate (for understand); biannual (for biennial); centre (for middle); centred around (for centred on); circle (for disc); continued (for continuous); degree (for extent); discreet (for discrete); either (for each or both); elicit (for illicit); especially (for specially); except (for unless); feel (for think); generally (for usually); if (for although); improvement (for alteration or change); lengthy (for long); limited (for few, small, slight or narrow); major (for great); minor (for little); natural (for normal); notable (for noticeable); optimistic (for hopeful); optimum (for highest); percentage (for some); practically (for almost); provided that (for if); quite (for entirely or rather); same (for similar); several (for some); singular or unique (for notable or rare); often (for in many places); sometimes (referring to place instead of time); superior (for better than); to (for too); transpire (for happen); view (for opinion); virtually (for almost); volume (for amount); weather (for climate); wastage (for waste); and while (for although, but or and). Consult a dictionary if you are uncertain of the meaning of any of these words.

Words may take on new meanings when people need to convey new ideas (or new words may be invented). The word broadcast used to mean the spreading of grains, but it is now used to mean the spreading of words – first by wireless (old word) and then by radio (a new word).

The meaning of words may change so much that they lose their value.

They no longer convey meaning precisely. The new use may remain incorrect or it may gradually gain acceptance. Consider the following words.

A *democracy* is a state practising government by the people, but this word has been abused by countries in which the citizens have no political rights.

Literally is a word that should be used rarely, if at all, by most writers. It means actually, and is usually superfluous or otherwise incorrect (see table 16). Literally means without exaggeration, yet it is commonly used in an attempt to affirm the truth of an exaggeration. For example: 'My eyes were literally glued to the television screen.'

Progress means a move forward, an improvement, a change from worse to better, but the word is misused for change of any kind. Indeed, the most outrageous suggestion may seem to acquire a certain respectability if someone calls it an improvement or progress. Consider, however, the monologue by Herbert Mundin (1926) about London's last cabby (cabman):

> It does not always happen
> That a change is for the good.
> More often it's the opposite
> I find.

Sophisticated was an uncomplimentary word, implying sophistry or artfulness, but it is now commonly used to mean complicated or to imply that a new instrument is in some way better than an earlier model. It is, in this context, an imprecise word that conveys no information.

Viable is a term which denotes the capacity to live, but in other contexts *not viable* may mean not competitive or will not work.

Vital means essential to life and this word should not be used in other contexts.

Words with only one meaning should not be qualified (see table 16). *Facts*, for example, are verified past events – things known to be true. It is wrong, therefore, to refer to the *fact* that energy *may* be involved, or to write that the *evidence* points to the *fact* or that someone has got his *facts wrong*, and to speak of the *actual facts* is to say the same thing twice (see table 15). Similarly, *unique* means the only one of its kind. Do not write *quite unique*: this is an unnecessary qualification of the word (see table 16). And perhaps those who write *almost unique* mean rare.

Table 15   *Tautology: saying the same thing twice using different words*

Tautology	Meaning
postponed to a later date	postponed
related to each other	related
still in use today	still in use
link together	link
percolate down	percolate
a tentative hypothesis	a hypothesis
ask the question whether	ask whether
on Friday 25 December next	on 25 December
the reason for this is because	because
in actual fact	in fact
one after another in succession	in succession
in the rural countryside	in the countryside
as an extra added bonus	as a bonus
my own personal opinion	my opinion
I tentatively suggest	I suggest
by advance planning	by planning
will disappear from sight	will disappear
in two equal halves	in halves
continue to remain	remain
symptoms indicative of	symptoms
a temporary loan	a loan
but . . . however	but *or* however
enclosed with this letter	enclosed
or alternatively	alternatively
equally as good	equally good *or* as good
an assassination attempt on the life of	an attempt on the life of
reverted back to woodland again	reverted to woodland
in the field of agriculture	in agriculture
each individual person	each person
every individual one	every one
may possibly go	may go
superimposed over each other	superimposed
grouped together	grouped
on pages 1–4 inclusive	on pages 1–4
from now on through until the end of December	until the end of December

Table 16 *The incorrect qualification of words*

Incorrect	Correct
absolutely perfect	perfect
in actual fact	in fact
they are in fact	they are
the actual number	the number
not actually true	untrue
a categorical denial	a denial
completely surrounded	surrounded
conclusive proof	proof
definitely correct	correct
deliberately avoided	avoided
an essential condition	a condition
facing up to	facing
they genuinely attempted	they attempted
genuinely sorry	sorry
hard evidence	evidence
limited in amount	small
streamlined in appearance	streamlined
hilly in character	hilly
blue in colour	blue
few in number	few
seasonal in occurrence	seasonal
stunted in growth	stunted
conical in shape	conical
small in size	small
literally impermeable	impermeable
positively rejected	rejected
quite correct	correct
quite unique	unique
a real pleasure	a pleasure
realistic justification	justification
they really are	they are
really dangerous	dangerous
really impossible	impossible
very real problems	problems
the smallest possible minimum	the minimum
very necessary	necessary
very relevant	relevant
very true	true
wholly new	new

The words of your subject

Easy communication between specialists depends upon their use of the special terms of their art, craft, or science: these are called technical terms. However, such terms may also be a barrier to communication. Students should show their understanding of the technical terms of their subject by using them correctly in appropriate contexts or, when necessary, by a precise and complete definition.

Specialists who hope to interest non-specialists should not use technical terms without explanation. And authors of textbooks should not introduce new words without defining them: they should appreciate that learning an additional vocabulary may be a considerable burden for anyone coming new to a subject, and should therefore present their subject as simply as they can.

When you write a technical term, you make two assumptions which are not always justified. You assume that the reader is familiar with the concept, and that he recognizes the concept by its technical name. Before using a technical term, therefore, you should consider whether or not it will help your readers. Technical terms should not be used unless they

Well . . . er . . . this is it.

Use words you expect your readers to understand.

are necessary: if possible an everyday word should be used if this can be done without affecting the meaning of the sentence. Furthermore, technical terms should not be used in an attempt to impress non-technical readers – or even your teachers.

However, you should appreciate the value of the special words of your subject, if you can use them correctly. Unless you can define these words and use them with accuracy and precision, you are handicapped in all your studies. See *Definitions*, p. 65.

You cannot understand any question in course work or examinations unless you are certain of the meaning of every word used in the question. Only then can you plan a complete and correct answer.

Examiners expect you to spell correctly, understand and if necessary define, the technical terms used in talking and writing about your subject. Every subject has technical terms, for example:

> *British constitution*: committee, constitution, government, politics, prorogation
>
> *Chemistry*: asymmetry, desiccate, fluorine, potassium, separate, soluble
>
> *Geology*: density, scenery, volcano
>
> *English literature*: descriptive, lyric, narrative skill, novel
>
> *History*: accession, dynasty, domestic, legislative
>
> *Music*: bar, bass, concerto, note, octave, serenade, sonata, symphony.

Consider the technical terms you use. Can you define them?

The examiner was not impressed by the candidate who, in a general studies paper, spelt satellite in eight ways in one essay – even though the correct spelling was given in the question.

In English literature students are expected to spell correctly the names of characters in the set book. And all students of European history should be able to spell proper names: Disraeli, Victor Emmanuel, Napoleon, and Peel, for example.

Abbreviations

Avoid abbreviations if you can. Like complete words, they must be understood by your reader. Remember that abbreviations which are commonly used in one country may not be understood in another, and also that one abbreviation may have several meanings, so that even after referring to a dictionary of abbreviations your reader may still not know which meaning you intended. Any essential abbreviation should be written in full when it is first used, and immediately abbreviated in parenthesis. Make sure you are consistent in using abbreviations and in their punctuation.

Try to convey your meaning without using phrases from another language, or even abbreviations of such phrases. Loc. cit. (in the place cited), op. cit. (in the work cited), and ibid. (in the same work), like the words 'former' and 'latter', may contribute to ambiguity. Even the abbreviations i.e. (*id est*: that is) and e.g. (*exempli gratia*: for example) are misused and, therefore, misunderstood by some people. Write 'namely' not *viz*, and 'about', not approximately, circa, ca., c., ~. The abbreviation etc. (*etcetera*: and other things), used at the end of a list, conveys no additional information, except that the list is incomplete. It is better to write 'for example' or 'including' immediately before the list.

These examples show the use of the full stop to indicate abbreviations. However, many abbreviations are not punctuated: for example, abbreviations which include the final letter of a word, such as Mr, Dr; or acronyms, such as WHO (World Health Organization) and ISO (International Standards Organization). Note particularly that punctuation marks should not be used with SI units (International System of Units, see p. 141). Another rule is that an s should not be added to an abbreviation, except in nos (numbers) and figs (figures in the sense of illustrations).

Improve your writing

1 *Consult a dictionary* whenever you come across a word that you do not understand. You will find this interesting and it will help you to increase the number of words at your command.

2 *Use a dictionary*, if necessary, to help you to distinguish between: adverse and averse, affectation and affection, aggravate and irritate, all together and altogether, allusion and illusion, anticipate and expect, beside and besides, born and borne, breath and breathe, canon and cannon, canvas and canvass, childish and childlike, dependant and dependent, deficient and defective, deprecate and depreciate, device and devise, discreet and discrete, except and accept, economic and economical, farther and further, formally and formerly, effective and efficient, eligible and illegible and ineligible, exceedingly and excessively, historic and historical, human and humane, industrial and industrious, illusion and allusion, imperial and imperious, implicit and explicit, ingenious and ingenuous, interfere and intervene, lightening and lightning, loose and lose, luxuriant and luxurious, marshal and martial, masterly and masterful, moral and morale, notable and noticeable, populace and popu-

lous, practicable and practical, practice and practise, precede and proceed, prescribe and proscribe, recourse and resource, reverend and reverent, review and revue, sceptic and septic, seasonable and seasonal, stationary and stationery, suspect and surmise, urban and urbane.

Try writing pairs of sentences using each word correctly in context.

3 *Words used in questions, in course work and examinations.* Consider carefully and make sure that you understand the precise meaning of each of the following words, used in questions: account, analyse, comment, compare, consider, define, describe, discuss, essay, evaluate, explain, illustrate, list, outline, review, state, and summarize. Many marks are lost by students who do not think carefully about the words used in the question before they start their answer.

Make sure that you understand the question. Answer the question that is asked. Respond to the precise wording of the question. The words used may tell you that the answer has to be in *a few words*, or *in your own words*, or *in full detail*. You may be asked to name *one* . . ., or to give *one* example of . . ., or to *assess* the relative importance of . . ., or to indicate *to what extent* . . ., or to state *how far*. . . .

You will get little credit for recalling and writing out all your notes on the subject of the question, or for writing all you know about any subject, if what you write is not an answer to the question.

4 *Definitions.* You may use a word in an appropriate context and yet have difficulty in defining it precisely. This is why examiners ask for definitions. When you have to define a word, note the points which must be included (like a topic outline) and then write your definition.

In any definition, proceed from the general to the particular. That is to say, state the general class to which the thing to be defined belongs (e.g. a *verb* is a word) and then the features which are peculiar to the thing defined (it is a word that indicates action). Your definition must be as simple as possible but it must apply to all instances of the thing defined; and it may be followed by an example. See table 27, p. 129.

5 *Exercises in comprehension.* Comprehension means understanding. Your understanding of any writing depends partly on the author's ability to express himself clearly and partly on your vocabulary. An exercise in comprehension is an attempt, by asking questions, to find out whether or not you understand the words and phrases used in a particular context. The questions should be answered concisely and in your own words.

The exercise stimulates thought and provides opportunities for discussion. You learn not only about writing but also about your subject. Exercises in comprehension may therefore be set by other teachers – of geography, history, or science, for example – as well as by teachers of English.

Every question set in course work and examinations is a test of your ability to understand. If you do not understand the exact meaning of the question you may answer the wrong question, or your answer may be incomplete.

7

Using words

In a dictionary, each word is first explained and then used in appropriate contexts to make its several meanings clear. For words do not stand alone: each word gives meaning to and takes meaning from the sentence, so that there is more to the whole than might be expected from its parts.

Words in context

Some people have favourite words and phrases – such as, also, apparently, case, found, incidentally, in fact, make, occur, of, perhaps, quite, show, and use. The use of a word twice in the same sentence, or several times in the same paragraph, or many times on the same page, may interrupt the smooth flow of language, and writers usually try to avoid such undue repetition. But do not be afraid to repeat a word if necessary. The right word should not be replaced by a less apt word for the sake of what is called elegant variation. Moreover, you may choose to repeat a word to emphasize an important point.

The position of a word in a sentence may also reflect the emphasis you wish to put upon it. An important word may, for example, come near the beginning or near the end, and in either position it may help to link the ideas expressed in successive sentences.

The position of a word may transform the meaning of a sentence. The word *only* is well known for the trouble it may cause when it is out of place. Putting it in the wrong place is partly attributable to custom, but is also a sign of carelessness. It is worth taking the trouble to be unambiguous (see table 17).

Table 17   *Examples of the word* only *out of place*

Extract	Meaning intended
The chemical was only manufactured in Europe.	The chemical was manufactured only in Europe.
The words no doubt should only be used when the idea of certainty is to be conveyed.	The words no doubt should be used only when the idea of certainty is to be conveyed.
I can only write well when I know what I want to say.	I can write well only when I know what I want to say.
It only works well for straight-forward pieces of descriptive writing.	It works well only for straight-forward pieces of descriptive writing.
He only made one journey which aroused the interest of detectives.	Only one of his journeys aroused the interest of detectives.
In this book those points of grammar only are discussed which will help you to ensure accuracy.	In this book only those points of grammar which will help you to ensure accuracy are discussed.

The words *this, that,* and *it (he* or *she)* and *one; former* and *latter;* and *other* and *another,* must be used with care or ambiguity may result. If necessary a noun should be repeated.

In writing at school or college, except in reporting conversation, it is best to use standard language and to avoid colloquial language and slang.

Standard English: written language or language used formally.

Colloquial English: usually spoken English (or language used informally – as between close friends). Except in reporting speech, colloquial English should not be used in writing. In particular, do not use such contractions as don't (do not), it's (it is) or they're (they are), and won't (will not), in course work or examinations.

Slang: highly colloquial language including new words or words used in a special sense.

In his *Usage and Abusage: a guide to good English* Eric Partridge (1965) gives, as an example of the difference: man (standard); chap (colloquial); and bloke, guy, stiff and bozo (slang).

If you are not sure whether or not a word is acceptable in writing, consult a dictionary:

bloke, n. (sl.). Fellow

chap, n. (colloq.). Fellow, boy or man.

These abbreviations are: n. = noun; sl. = slang; colloq. = colloquial. The words fellow, boy and man are standard English.

In writing at school or college it is also best to avoid clichés (see p. 54) and idiomatic expressions (see table 18). In idiomatic expressions the words have a special meaning which might not be understood by some of your readers.

Table 18   *Avoid idiomatic expressions*

Idiomatic expression	Meaning
explore every avenue	consider all possibilities
break new ground	start something new
it goes without saying	obviously
read between the lines	understand more than is said or written
in the pipeline	being prepared
work against time	try to finish in the time available

Ready-made phrases make less impact than does something new. They indicate that the writer has not troubled to choose words that convey his meaning precisely. In *Politics and the English Language*, George Orwell (1950) wrote:

As soon as certain topics are raised . . . no one seems able to think of turns of speech that are not hackneyed: prose consists less and less of *words* chosen for the sake of their meaning, and more and more of *phrases* tacked together like the sections of a prefabricated hen-house.

In this way, people deny themselves the simple pleasure of putting their own thoughts into their own words. Instead, always:

> Open a new window,
> Open a new door.
> Travel a new highway
> That's never been tried before.
> *Mame*, Lyric by Jerry Herman (1966)

Superfluous words

Using too many words is a more common fault in writing than using the wrong word; and while summarizing and qualifying phrases may help your readers (see also comment words and connectives, p. 77), any unnecessary words can only confuse, distract and annoy. A well constructed sentence should have neither too many words nor too few: each word should be there for a purpose.

'I cut out only necessary words'

In your writing cut out all unnecessary words.

In his book *On the Art of Writing* (1916), Sir Arthur Quiller Couch condemned jargon and gave the following advice. (1) Prefer transitive verbs and use them in the active voice. For example, write 'we obtained the following information' not 'the following information was obtained' (see also, table 21). (2) Prefer concrete nouns (things that you can touch and see) to abstract nouns. (3) Prefer the direct word to the circumlocution (see tables 19 and 20).

Quiller Couch listed words that should be used *sparingly and with care* by those who wish to avoid jargon: case, instance, character, nature, condition, persuasion, and degree. Other indicators of jargon are: area, angle, aspect, fact, field, level, situation, spectrum, time, and type (see tables 12, 19 and 20). Of course there is nothing wrong with any of these words if you need them to convey your meaning.

Many introductory phrases and connectives can be deleted without altering the meaning of the sentence (see table 11 and table 12). If you are in the habit of using such phrases, cut them out and your writing will be more direct, easier to read, and therefore more effective in conveying your meaning.

Table 19 *Circumlocution: the use of many words where fewer would be better*

Circumlocution	Better English
Is this a temporary situation or is it permanent?	Is this temporary?
There was a large measure of agreement.	Most people agreed.
not more than 20,000 to 25,000 words in length	no more than 25,000 words
a disproportionate number	too few, *or* few, *or* many, *or* too many (?)
ten metres in length	ten metres long
for a further period of fifteen years	for another fifteen years
the roads were limited in mileage	there were few roads
if at all possible	if possible
an oral presentation	a talk
on a dawn to dusk basis	from dawn to dusk
I would have thought	I think
I myself would hope	I hope
you are in fact quite correct	you are right
during the month of April	in April
in the field of medicine	in medicine
in the school environment	in schools
on the educational front	in education
at the pre-school level	the under-fives
Such is by no means the case.	This is not so.
The standard of English was poor in most cases.	The English of most candidates was poor.
In the case of the fifth question	in answering the fifth question
We are continuing to review the situation on a day to bay basis.	We review the situation daily.
They are without any sanitary arrangements whatsoever.	There is no sanitation.
there is really somewhat of an obligation upon us	we ought
we are actually in the process of examining	we are examining

a lot of information condensed into a very little amount of space	a lot of information in a small space
few candidates were not in a position to offer	most candidates offered
no admittance to unauthorized personnel	No admittance

Table 20   *Circumlocution: some phrases which should not be used if one word would be better*

Circumlocution	Better English	Circumlocution	Better English
it would appear that	apparently	for the purpose of	for
due to the fact that	because	aimed at	for
it is apparent	hence	if it is assumed that	if
therefore that		in the event that	if
in all other cases	otherwise	with the exception of	except
it may well be that	perhaps	entertainment value	fun
by the same token	similarly	in the vicinity of	near
with the result that	so	a sufficient number of	enough
in the process of	building	a small number of	few
building		a large number of	many
which goes under the name of	called	a large majority of	most
		a high degree of	much
has an ability to	can	a great deal of	much
is not in a position to	cannot	a number of	several
		a proportion of	some
in connection with	about	prior to	before
with regard to	about	if and when	if (or when)
in between	between	at a later date	later
using a combination of	from	later on	later
in the nature of	like	a greater length of time	longer
in order to	to		
in conjunction with	with	at the present time	now
in spite of the fact that	although	at this precise moment in time	now
to say nothing of	and	on a regular basis	regularly
on account of the fact that	as	have been shown to be	are
		check on	check
make an adjustment to	adjust	take into consideration	consider
afford an opportunity to	allow	come to the conclusion that	conclude

count up	count	at that point in time	then
arrive at a decision	decide	after this has been done	then
give positive encouragement to	encourage	in this day and age	today
make an examination of	examine	on two separate occasions	twice
spell out in depth	explain	until such time as	until
bring to a conclusion	finish	in most cases	usually
conduct an investigation into	investigate	during the time that	while
it must be remembered that	remember	dusty in character	dusty
		somewhat costly	expensive
seal off	seal	of a reversible nature	reversible
undertake a study of	study	in view of the following	therefore
try out	try		
make an attempt to	try	are found to be in agreement	agree
proved to be	were		
at an early date	soon	open up	open

Circumlocution – verbosity – gobbledegook – surplusage – this habit of excess in the use of words, which makes communication more difficult than is necessary, is well established in the speech and writing of many people:

> . . . of all the Studies of men, nothing may be sooner obtain'd than this vicious abundance of *Phrase*, this trick of *Metaphors*, this volubility of *Tongue*, which makes so great a noise in the World. But I spend words in vain; for the evil is now so inveterate, that it is hard to know whom to *blame*, or where to begin to *reform*. We all value one another so much, upon this beautiful deceit; and labour for so long after it, in the years of our education: that we cannot but ever after think kinder of it, than it deserves.
>
> *The History of the Royal Society*, Thomas Sprat (1667)

Reasons for verbosity

Tautology, circumlocution and verbosity arise from ignorance of the exact meaning of words. Also, people may use two many words, or too few, if they have not considered the difference between speech and writing.

Human communication, it sometimes seems to me, involves an exaggerated amount of time. How briefly and to the point people always seem to speak on the stage or on the screen, while in real life we stumble from phrase to phrase with endless repetition.

Travels with My Aunt, Graham Greene (1969)

Sometimes in conversation we use more words than would be needed in writing. We use words to separate important ideas; we repeat things for emphasis; and we correct ourselves as we talk – in an attempt to achieve greater precision. These things give the listener time to think. We hesitate and this gives us time to think.

In conversation we use gestures and facial expressions. As we talk we see that the listener has grasped our meaning. We may therefore use fewer words than would be needed in writing.

In writing we must allow for the lack of direct contact with the reader. Meaning is conveyed by words alone, and we must use as many words as are needed to convey our thoughts precisely. On the one hand, therefore, more words may be necessary than in conversation. On the other hand, repetition can usually be avoided because the writer has time to plan and to revise his first thoughts, and the reader can move at his own pace. Necessary pauses come from punctuation marks and paragraph breaks.

The writer . . . suggests by turns of expression the emphasis and gestures of ordinary talk; uses vocabulary that is at once intelligible, interesting and evocative; and so varies his constructions that he avoids the effect of monotony. He gives coherence to speech, at the same time retaining certain of its characteristics. His immediate appeal is through the eye of the reader, but he does not forget the reader's ear.

The Best English, G. H. Vallins (1960)

Use words with which you are familiar and try to match your style to the occasion and to the needs of your readers. Write as you would speak but recognize that good spoken English is not the same as good written English. If a good talk is recorded and then typed, the reader may find that it is not good prose.

If they are prepared to take the trouble, most people should be able to write better than they can talk, because in writing there is more time for thought and there is the opportunity for revision.

Apart from failure to consider the difference between speech and writing, there are other reasons why people fill their writing with empty words. Some writers seem to think that restatement in longer words is explanation. Others are trying to make a little knowledge go a long way, or they may be trying to obscure meaning because they have nothing to say, or because they do not wish to commit themselves:

'Do, as a concession to my poor wits, Lord Darlington, just explain to me what you really mean.'

'I think I had better not, Duchess. Nowadays to be intelligible is to be found out.'

> *Lady Windermere's Fan*, Oscar Wilde (1892)

. . . only the wealthy, the capable, or the pretty can afford the luxury of saying right out just what they think, and blow the consequences.

> *Lieutenant Bones*, Edgar Wallace (1918)

Wordiness may also result from affectation – from the studied avoidance of simplicity – in the belief that Latin phrases, long words and elaborate sentences, appear learned.

Foreign words and expressions . . . are used to give an air of culture and elegance. The ends of sentences are saved from anti-climax by such resounding commonplaces as *greatly to be desired, cannot be left out of account, a development to be expected in the near future, deserving of serious consideration*, and *brought to a satisfactory conclusion*. Words like phenomenon, element, individual (as a noun), objective, categorical, effective, virtual, basic, primary, promote, constitute, exhibit, exploit, utilize, eliminate, liquidate, are used to dress up simple statement and give an air of scientific impartiality to biased judgements.

> *Politics and the English Language*, George Orwell (1950)

Orwell recommends those who wish to use language as an instrument for expressing and not for concealing thought, to:

1 Be positive. Especially, avoid double negatives such as *not unlikely* (for possible) and *not unjustifiable*.
2 Never use a metaphor, simile or other figure of speech which you are used to seeing in print.
3 Never use a long word where a short one will do.
4 Never use a foreign phrase, a scientific word or a jargon word if you can think of an everyday English equivalent.
5 If it is possible to cut a word out, always cut it out.
6 Never use the passive where you can use the active.

The use of the passive enables the author to avoid the first person. The repeated use of *I* or *we* is undesirable, but some authors consider it impolite to refer to oneself directly and may go to great lengths (be verbose) in attempting to avoid doing so. Also, the editors of most scientific journals insist on the use of the passive: 'Measurements were made', not 'I measured' or 'We measured'. However, the first person is more direct and it can make a communication more personal and more forceful (table 21).

Table 21   *Examples of the use of the active and passive voice*

Prefer the active voice to the . . .	passive voice
We all have to read a mass of papers.	A mass of papers have to be read.
I ask my colleagues and their staffs to . . .	My colleagues and their staffs are asked to . . .

The following memorandum was written by Winston Churchill in 1940 to the heads of all government departments.

To do our work, we all have to read a mass of papers. Nearly all of them are far too long. This wastes time, while energy has to be spent in looking for the essential points.

I ask my colleagues and their staffs to see to it that their Reports are shorter.

(i) The aim should be Reports which set out the main points in a series of short, crisp paragraphs.

(ii) If a Report relies on detailed analysis of some complicated factors, or on statistics, these should be set out in an Appendix.

(iii) Often the occasion is best met by submitting not a full-dress Report, but an *Aide-memoire* consisting of headings only, which can be expanded orally if needed.

(iv) Let us have an end of such phrases as these: 'It is also of importance to bear in mind the following considerations . . .', or 'Consideration should be given to the possibility of carrying into effect . . .'. Most of these woolly phrases are mere padding, which can be left out altogether, or replaced by a single word. Let us not shrink from using the short expressive phrase, even if it is conversational.

Reports drawn up on the lines I propose may at first sight seem rough as compared with the flat surface of officialese jargon. But the saving in time will be great, while the discipline of setting out the real points concisely will prove an aid to clearer thinking.

Simplicity is the outward sign of clarity of thought. Wordiness is therefore a reflection on a writer's thinking; and a means by which he conceals his meaning – perhaps even from himself.

If men would only say what they have to say in plain terms how much more eloquent they would be.

On Style, Samuel Coleridge (1772–1834)

Anyone who wishes to become a good writer should endeavour, before he allows himself to be tempted by the more showy qualities, to be direct, simple, brief, vigorous and lucid.

The King's English, H. W. Fowler and F. G. Fowler (1939)

We shall be effective . . . as writers if we can say clearly, simply, and attractively just what we want to say and nothing more. If we really have something worth saying, then we are bound by the nature and necessities of our language to say it as simply as we can.

Our Language, Simeon Potter (1966)

In practising an economy of words, do not make the mistake of using too few words. Include comment words (such as *even, dangerously, as expected,* and *unexpected*) and connecting words (such as *hence, however, moreover, nevertheless, on the contrary,* and *therefore*) to direct your reader's attention.

Do not pack important thoughts so closely that your reader has no time to grasp the full meaning of one before the next is upon him. Provide reminders when these are needed. Your subject should not be drowned in a sea of words, nor starved of the words needed to give it strength. The rule must be to use the number of words needed to convey a thought precisely (without ambiguity). Brevity must not be achieved at the expense of clarity, accuracy, interest and coherence.

Improve your writing

The ability to write précis and summaries will be useful when you take notes and when you wish to incorporate information and ideas, from any source, in one of your own compositions (see p. 108). As an employee you will need to select carefully if you wish, for example, to inform other people in the same organization of the relevant parts of an article or report. What you consider to be the essentials will depend upon why you are writing and for whom you are writing.

1 *How to write a précis*. If you have little experience of précis writing it is

advisable to read the original more than once before you start your précis. Read first to make sure that you understand every sentence. Read again, using your judgement and selecting the main points: as you note these you are reconstructing the author's topic outline. Decide the author's purpose and then choose an effective heading for your précis. Keep this heading in mind as you make a rough draft based on your notes. Check your précis against the original, making sure that the writer of the original is acknowledged and accurately reported.

With practice you will grasp the essentials of a composition at first reading and you will find précis writing easier. The précis must be in good English, not in note form. The order of presentation should not be changed, unless the order is faulty. Remember that you are conveying the author's meaning accurately but in fewer words. Omit all figurative language or ornament, anything of secondary importance, and all digressions and superfluous words.

Regular practice in précis writing helps students to learn aspects of effective study: *careful reading* and *comprehension*, the *exercise of judgement* in *selecting* the essentials, and *accurate reporting*. Preparing a précis should also help students to learn more about selected aspects of their subject. Suitable exercises may therefore be set by teachers of other subjects, and not just by teachers of English.

Students may help themselves by practising the technique of précis writing. For example, you might try writing a précis of a leading article from a newspaper or of an article from a magazine or journal. Also, rewrite one of your own essays: try to reduce its length by 25 or 50 per cent.

2 *How to write a summary.* A summary differs from a précis in that it should be as short as possible. The summary of an article includes only the main points. It is like a topic outline but is written in complete sentences, not in note form. Preparing a summary is a useful exercise for students, and they may find it useful to incorporate summaries of things they read at appropriate points in their own notes (see p. 99). However, your own compositions in course work and examinations will mostly be too short to require a summary.

The difference between a précis and a summary should be clear from the following examples: a précis of an extract from *Human Biology*, a 'Made Simple' book published by William Heinemann, London; and a summary of the same extract.

Précis

Smoking or health?

Tobacco smoke contains many harmful chemicals, including the drug nicotine – on which smokers become dependent – and carbon monoxide which reduces the oxygen-carrying capacity of the blood. This causes smokers to become breathless quickly during exercise and increases the risk of a heart attack. The smoke also contains cancer-inducing chemicals and irritants that make smokers cough and cause bronchitis.

In Britain, more than twice as many smokers as non-smokers, aged thirty-five and over, die before the age of sixty-five. Since the danger to health first received publicity, many doctors have stopped smoking and deaths of doctors before the age of sixty-five, from diseases aggravated by smoking, have fallen by 21 per cent. But in the general population, who are not so well informed, deaths from smokers' diseases before the age of sixty-five have fallen by only 7 per cent.

Summary

Tobacco smoke contains harmful chemicals that cause drug-dependence, shortage of breath during exercise, heart attacks, smokers' cough, bronchitis, and cancer. Since this was established many people are living longer because they have stopped smoking.

8

Helping your readers

By making things easy for your readers, you help yourself to convey information and ideas. You should therefore find out as much as you can about your readers and try to match your vocabulary and style of writing to their needs. This is easiest if you are a student writing for one reader, or an employee writing to a colleague.

Try to anticipate your readers' difficulties so that your writing can be understood at first reading by all those for whom it is intended.

Provide an informative title and, if appropriate, use headings and sub-headings as sign posts. Present information in a logical order; include all essential steps in any argument; give sufficient evidence in support of anything new; give examples, and explain why any point is particularly important. No statement should be self-evident, but be as explicit as is necessary. Do not leave your readers to work out the implications of any statement. Help them to see the logical connection between sentences and paragraphs. Sometimes a word or phrase is enough; sometimes much more explanation is required.

Try not to mislead your readers. Make clear any assumptions under-lying your arguments, because if these were incorrect your conclusions might also be incorrect. Take care that any assumptions, conjectures or possibilities are not later referred to as if they were facts. Words to watch, because they may introduce an opinion, are *obviously, surely,* and *of course* (see also table 12).

Fulfil your readers' expectations. For example, follow the words *not only* by *but also; whether* by *or; on the one hand* by *on the other hand;* and *first(ly)* by *second(ly).* If you list a number of items, mention all or none of them in the sentences that follow: if only some are mentioned, your readers may wonder about the others when they should be thinking about your next topic.

Write for easy reading

Your writing should be appropriate to the subject, to the needs of your readers and to the occasion. Convey your thoughts clearly, accurately and impartially so that your readers take your meaning and always feel at ease.

How to begin

If you know what you wish to communicate but have difficulty in getting started, look at the opening sentences of similar compositions by other people. You might begin, for example, with a question or with an answer to one of your readers' six questions (who, what, where, when, why or how). The best starting point, for the subject and for your readers, will usually become apparent as you prepare your topic outline. However, it is better to get started than to spend too much time trying to think of the most effective beginning. The only rules are: (1) leave no doubt about the purpose and scope of the composition – and in course work and examinations make clear that you understand the terms used in the question and the meaning of the question; (2) make your first paragraph short and to the point (see emphasis, p. 83); and (3) start with things that you expect your readers to know and build on this foundation.

Control

Try to maintain the momentum of your writing. Do not dwell for too long on any topic, therefore, and make the connection between paragraphs clear. Apply the test of relevance to everything. Make sure that every word or phrase is appropriate to its context and that every sentence conveys a whole thought.

Good headings (see p. 42) and paragraph breaks help the reader along – but only if the headings and paragraphs are in a logical sequence which is obvious to the reader. Keeping control, therefore, depends upon your knowledge of the subject and upon careful planning (see p. 42) which enables you to deal fully with each topic in one place and to present your thoughts in an appropriate, ordered and interesting way.

The use of tables. Tables are useful, especially in extended essays and project reports (see p. 107), because they allow you to provide additional relevant information without interrupting the flow of words. The information presented in tables should not, therefore, be repeated elsewhere.

Each table should be numbered, appropriately placed, and have a clear and concise heading. There should be at least one reference to the table in your composition; but it should be possible to understand the table without reading the text (see table 22).

The first column on the left identifies the horizontal lines. Each column should have a concise heading in which units are stated for every quantity shown. If there is no entry in any particular part of the table, this should be shown by three dots . . . and a footnote to indicate that no information is available.

Any necessary footnotes should be immediately below the table to which they apply, but there should be no other writing on the same page. Each footnote should be preceded by a letter or symbol (not by a number) which must also be included in the table to identify the entry to which the footnote refers.

Table 22   *Information presented concisely without interrupting the flow of words in the text. (See also Figs 3 to 5)*

	WORLD		
	Population (millions)		Surface area[a] km² 000's
Date	1950	1975	
Africa	219	406	30 338
America[b]	330	559	42 082
Asia[c]	1 380	2 319	27 580
Europe[c]	392	474	4 937
Oceania	12.6	21.2	8 510
USSR	180	254	22 402
World totals[d]	2,513	4,033	135,849

Notes
(a)   including unproductive land
(b)   including Hawaii
(c)   USSR shown separately
(d)   all estimates from *United Nations Demographic Year Book*

Emphasis

In speech, emphasis is achieved mainly by inflexions of the voice. In writing, mark the points that you wish to emphasize in your topic outline, so that you can ensure that they are sufficiently emphasized in your finished composition. There are many ways in which, without the sound of your voice, you can draw a reader's attention to parts of a composition, particular sentences in a paragraph, and selected words in a sentence.

The title and any headings and sub-headings serve to emphasize the purpose of the whole and its parts. See pages 41 and 42.

Emphasis is important in all writing and is present whether or not the writer is in control. But a writer can use emphasis effectively only if he knows how to make important points stand out from the supporting detail.

Devote one paragraph to each topic. Paragraphs are units of thought and will therefore vary in length (see p. 46). However, if the topics are of comparable importance, you might expect to write paragraphs of similar length.

Plan effective diagrams if these will help you to convey the essential points of your composition (see p. 32), or if they are necessary to enable you to convey information that cannot be conveyed by words alone.

Beginnings and endings are most important. The first and last paragraphs (the introduction and conclusion, see pages 44 and 46) are those to which readers pay most attention. The most important words in each paragraph are the first words (so miss out unnecessary introductory phrases, see tables 11 and 12) and the last words (so end each paragraph effectively).

The most important words in a sentence, for emphasis, come at the beginning and at the end. The first words direct the reader's attention. The writer may use the same words to convey the same information and yet affect the reader differently, because the words that come first are emphasized. For example:

The first men on the moon were two United States astronauts, Neil Armstrong and Edward Aldrin.

Two United States astronauts, Neil Armstrong and Edward Aldrin, were the first men on the moon.

Neil Armstrong and Edward Aldrin, two United States astronauts, were the first men on the moon.

Asides, within a sentence, may be marked – according to the importance you place upon them – by commas, parentheses or dashes (as in this sentence). (See also dash and parenthesis, p. 133.)

You may underline words in your topic outline or in your notes to draw attention to the most important points, but in a composition emphasis should normally be achieved without underlining. Underline only the words which, in books, would be printed in italics: conjuctions such as <u>but</u>, <u>and</u>, <u>either</u> . . . <u>or</u>, and <u>neither</u> . . . <u>nor</u>, when used – as in many examination questions – to make an important distinction or contrast; the titles of books, plays and poems; the names of newspapers, magazines and journals; the scientific names of organisms (e.g. <u>Hamlet</u>, <u>The Times</u> and <u>Homo sapiens</u>); and words from a foreign language.

Leave out anything that is irrelevant, not only because irrelevant material wastes everyone's time but also because you must take care not to draw the reader's attention away from relevant material. Use more forceful language for important points than for the supporting detail. Repeat important words.

Items of comparable importance may be emphasized *by* repeating an introductory word (as in this sentence), *by* numbering (as on p. 85), or *by* indentation (see the quotations on p. 89). However, if a sentence or paragraph is well balanced, so that it reads well, emphasis will fall naturally on each part.

Long, involved sentences may indicate that you have not thought sufficiently about what you wish to say. However, if it is properly constructed, a long sentence may be easier to read than a succession of short ones. There is no rule that a sentence, when read aloud, should be read in one breath.

For the beginner, short sentences are easiest to write and easiest to read, but good prose is seldom written entirely in short sentences. Sentences vary in length. Short sentences are effective for introducing a new topic (as in two of the preceding twelve paragraphs), long sentences for developing a point, and short ones for emphasizing each step in an argument or, as in the quotation that follows, for bringing things to a striking conclusion.

> 'If you really want to know,' said Mr Shaw with a sly twinkle, 'I think that he who was so willing and able to prove that what was, was not, would be equally able and willing to make a case for thinking that what was not, was, if it suited his purpose.' Ernest was very much taken aback.
>
> *The Way of All Flesh*, Samuel Butler (1903)

The breaks between sentences give time for thought; Rudolph Flesch (1962), in *The Art of Plain Talk*, grades writing, according to *average* sentence length, as very easy to read (less than 10 words), difficult (more than 20 words) and very difficult (more than 30 words). Accept this as a guide, and match your sentence length to the needs of your readers.

Rhythm

Well-written prose has a varied rhythm that contrasts with the strict metred rhythm of verse, and yet contributes to the flow of words in a sentence. With the flow of logically arranged thoughts in successive sentences, this helps to make a passage interesting and easy to read. Rhythm may give emphasis and help to present shades of meaning.

Use punctuation marks to clarify meaning and to contribute to the smooth flow of language. Effective prose usually sounds well, and a good test of your writing is to read it aloud to see if it is easy to read. McCartney (1953), in his *Recurrent Maladies of Scholarly Writing*, suggests that writers with a feeling for euphony (the sounds of words) try not to offend the ear:

1 by unintentional alliteration, as in *rather regularly radial;*
2 by the grating repetition of s, as in *such a sense of success;*
3 by adding s to a word that does not require it, such as *toward* and *forward* (but the s may be needed to make the sentence easier to read);
4 by the repetition of syllables, as in *appropriate approach;*
5 by the repetition of sound, as in *found around;*
6 by the repetition of cognate forms in different parts of speech, as in a *locality located,* and *except for rare exceptions;* and
7 by repeating a word with a change of meaning, as in *a point to point out.*

Style

You cannot add style to writing, as a final polish, because it is part of effective prose. Jonathan Swift defined style as *proper words in proper places,* and Matthew Arnold considered that the secret of style is *to have something to say and to say it as simply as you can.*

Graves and Hodge (1947), in *The Reader Over Your Shoulder,* suggest that the style of prose best suited to the present day should be:

1 Cleared of encumbrances for quick reading; that is, without un-necessary ornament, irrelevancy, illogicality, ambiguity, repetition, circumlocution, obscurity of reference.
2 Properly laid out; that is, with each sentence a single step and each

paragraph a complete stage in the argument or narrative; with each idea in its right place in the sequence, and none missing; with all connections properly made.

3 Written in the first place for silent reading, but with consideration for euphony if read aloud.

4 Consistent in use of language; considerate of the possible limitations of the reader's knowledge; with no indulgence of personal caprice nor any attempt to improve on sincere statement by rhetorical artifice.

The need for careful planning is emphasized in these notes on style, and in George de Buffon's address to the Académie Française in 1703:

> This plan is not indeed the style, but it is the foundation; it supports the style, directs it, governs its movement, and subjects it to law. Without a plan, the best writer will lose his way. His pen will run on unguided and by hazard will make uncertain strokes and incorrect figures. Style is but the order and the movement that one gives to one's thoughts.

A good style depends upon your intelligence, imagination and good taste; upon sincerity, modesty and careful planning. Rhythm, while not essential, will make for easier reading, and badly constructed sentences may irritate readers and make them less receptive to your message.

Capture and hold your reader's interest

A novelist, whose business is words, must quickly capture and hold the reader's interest. He takes great care over the choice and use of words. Consider, for example, the first paragraph of a successful novel:

> He rode into our valley in the summer of '89. I was a kid then, barely topping the backboard of father's old chuckwagon. I was on the upper rail of our small corral, soaking in the late afternoon sun, when I saw him far down the road where it swung into the valley from the open plain beyond.
>
> *Shane*, Jack Schaeffer (1954)

The first two words capture the reader's attention. The first sentence (in ten short words) tells what the story is about; it begins to answer the reader's questions – who, where, and when? The first paragraph tells that the story will be told as it affected the life of a small boy. No word is superfluous. Each one plays a part in setting the scene.

Note how interest is maintained in a newspaper report; by reference to familiar things, and by examples, anecdotes and analogies. Harold Evans in *Newsman's English*, Vol. 1 (1972) emphasizes that:

> Newspapers are short of space and their readers are short of time. The language must be concise, emphatic and to the point. Every word must be understood by the ordinary man, every sentence must be clear at a glance, and every story must say something about people.

Newsman's English includes a number of editing exercises in which Evans removes superfluous words and rearranges the information to make each story more direct and more interesting to the reader.

How to make your writing interesting

Approach your readers through their interests rather than your own. Remember that people are most interested in themselves, in other people, and in things as they affect people.

To maintain interest, you must present information at a proper pace. If readers understand they will want to move quickly to the point. However, they must understand every word, every statement, and every step in any argument; for if they must consult a dictionary or read a sentence twice, to confirm that they have taken the right meaning, their attention may be lost.

Use comment words and connecting words (see p. 77) to help your reader to move smoothly from one thought to the next. Readers are directed away from your explanation or argument by anything that is not relevant, by unnecessary detail, by the explanation of the obvious (but see p. 43), or by needless repetition.

When anything is repeated, for emphasis or to help to clarify a difficult point, use a phrase such as *that is to say* or *in other words*. Otherwise, after studying both sentences to make sure that their meaning is the same, readers may still wonder if they have failed to appreciate some difference.

Improve your writing

1 *Use good English*. Mistakes in grammar make writing inaccurate, imprecise and ambiguous. Grammar (the art of speaking, reading and writing correctly) is not therefore something that can be ignored: it may be acquired subconsciously by those who speak well and read good prose; or it may be learned with effort from a teacher of English or by studying a textbook on the English language – and by reading good prose.

2 *Read good prose.* In starting to play any game, it is a good idea to watch an expert. Similarly, in learning to write effectively, it is helpful to study the technique of the successful writer.

Evelyn Waugh (see also p. 7) advised a young writer to read the works of sixteenth-, seventeenth- and nineteenth-century authors. W. Somerset Maugham, in *The Summing Up* (1938) commends the prose of John Dryden (1631–1700), Joseph Addison (1672–1719), Jonathan Swift (1667–1745), William Hazlitt (1778–1830), John Henry Newman (1801–90) and Matthew Arnold (1822–88). Maugham (see also p. 6 and p. 40) considers the two most important qualities in writing to be clarity and simplicity, but regrets that:

> English prose is elaborate rather than simple. It was not always so. Nothing could be more racy, straightforward, and alive than the prose of Shakespeare; . . . To my mind King James's Bible has had a harmful influence . . . There are passages of a simplicity that is deeply moving. But it is an oriental book. Its alien imagery has nothing to do with us. Those hyperboles, those luscious metaphors, are foreign to our genius.

Some of the most successful British and American writers, in every age, have expressed themselves clearly and simply. Francis Bacon (1561–1626) in *Of Studies*, an essay, wrote:

> Read not to contradict and confute, nor to believe and take for granted, nor to find talk and discourse, but to weigh and consider. . . . some books are to be read only in parts; others to be read but not curiously; and some few to be read wholly, and with diligence and attention.

In *As You Like It*, written in 1601, William Shakespeare wrote some of the best-known lines in the English language, in words that are still easily understood by all English-speaking people.

> All the world's a stage,
> And all the men and women merely players:
> They have their exits, and their entrances;
> And one man in his time plays many parts,
> His acts being in seven ages. At first . . .

Joseph Addison (1672–1719) in *A Citizen's Diary*, an essay, gave clear advice that is still easy to read and worth considering.

I would, however, recommend to every one of my readers, the keeping a journal of their lives for one week, and setting down punctually their whole series of employment during that space of time. This kind of examination would give them a true state of themselves and incline them to consider seriously what they are about.

In *Robinson Crusoe*, the first English novel, published in 1719, Daniel Defoe wrote one of the best known passages in English prose. Note the clear, direct and simple style.

> . . . one day about noon going towards my boat, I was exceedingly surprised with the print of a man's naked foot on the shore, which was very plain to be seen in the sand. I stood like one thunderstruck, or as if I had seen an apparition; . . .

Thomas Jefferson (1743–1826) wrote *The Declaration of Independence* of the United States of America, which begins:

> When in the Course of human events, it becomes necessary for one people to dissolve the political bands, which have connected them with another, and to assume among the powers of the earth, the separate and equal station to which the Laws of Nature and of Nature's God entitle them, a decent respect to the opinions of mankind requires that they should declare the causes which impel them to the separation.

The continuing appeal of the Declaration is due not only to its expression of the feelings of a people but also to Jefferson's clear and simple style.

William Hazlitt (1778–1830) in an essay *On the Ignorance of the Learned* wrote concisely and gave good advice to students.

> It is better to be able neither to read nor write than to be able to do nothing else. . . . Learning is, in too many cases, but a foil to common sense; a substitute for true knowledge. Books are less often made use of as 'spectacles' to look at nature with, than as blinds to keep out its strong light and shifting scenery from weak eyes and indolent dispositions.

Robert Louis Stephenson (1850–94) in *An Apology for Idlers*, an essay, emphasized the need for relaxation and the importance of everyday experiences.

> I have attended a good many lectures in my time. I still remember that the spinning of a top is a case of Kinetic Stability. I still

remember that Emphyteusis is not a disease, nor Stillicide a crime. But though I would not willingly part with such scraps of science, I do not set the same store by them as by certain other odds and ends that I came by in the open street . . .

Sir Arthur Bryant wrote a weekly Note Book in the *Illustrated London News* for more than thirty years. He wrote in clear and simple English; and in *The Lion and The Unicorn* (1969) he emphasized that the successful author must capture the interest of his readers.

If anyone wonders why my column in the *Illustrated London News* has any readers, I can only suggest the answer King Charles II gave when asked to explain how a particularly stupid clergyman, whom he had made a bishop, had converted his flock from dissent to orthodoxy: 'I suppose his sort of nonsense suits their sort of nonsense!'

Young writers, still developing a style of their own, will find clear, simple and straightforward prose in, for example, books by Samuel Butler (see p. 84), Winston Churchill (see pp. 4 and 76), Robert Graves

'. . . the print of a man's naked foot . . . in the sand. I stood like one thunderstuck . . .'

To write well most people need to be left alone, free from distraction, with time for thought.

(see pp. 12 and 85), George Orwell (see p. 75), Dorothy L. Sayers (see p. 4), and H. G. Wells (see p. 13).

Read for pleasure. Without effort, as a result, you will find that your writing improves. Read widely, and you will find that successful authors do not waste words.

> Mr Stevens sat with his map on his knees, because he liked to pick out the distant church spires and name the clustering houses. He liked to find on the map the streams he would cross before they came in sight. He was fond of maps, and had learnt to read them well. They appealed to him because of the endless pleasure they offered his imagination, the picture they showed him of a country built up through the romantic casualness of centuries.
>
> *The Fortnight in September*, R. C. Sherriff (1931)

Just as the way we speak is influenced by the speech we hear, so our writing is influenced by the prose we read. The King James I Bible had a profound effect on speech and writing when it was the staple literature of English-speaking people, just as our daily newspapers do now. Most people read newspapers, and some read nothing else. Journalists and broadcasters use the English of today and may have an untold influence on the development of our language.

3 *Read good newspapers.* Readers of newspapers look first for things that are of interest; and they read only things that they can understand. Different newspapers are written to appeal to people with different views on politics; or to convert readers to a particular point of view. They are also intended to be understood by people who differ in intelligence. Look carefully at different newspapers to see if you can detect their political bias. In papers that you think are for more intelligent or better educated readers what do you notice about the length of paragraphs, sentences and words in comparison with papers written for less intelligent readers?

Because your vocabulary and style of writing are influenced by the things you read, it is best to read a good newspaper. Study the technique of journalists who write well, in feature articles and in leading articles especially, to see how to capture your readers' attention, how to inform, how to express a point of view, how to persuade, how to match your writing to the needs of your readers, and how to write a clear, concise, vigorous and vivid prose.

However, it is a mistake to try to copy someone else's style. There is no one correct way to write, because the way each person puts words together to convey meaning reflects his personality and his feeling for words.

Leonard was trying to form his style on Ruskin: he understood him to be the greatest master of English Prose. He read forward steadily, occasionally making a few notes.

'Let us consider a little each of these characters in succession, and first (for of the shafts enough has been said already), what is very peculiar to this church – its luminousness.'

Was there anything to be learnt from this fine sentence? Could he adapt it to the needs of daily life? Could he introduce it, with modifications, when he next wrote a letter to his brother, the lay reader? For example:

'Let us consider a little each of these characters in succession, and first (for of the absence of ventilation enough has been said already), what is very peculiar to this flat – its obscurity.'

Something told him that the modification would not do, and that something, had he known it, was the spirit of English Prose. 'My flat is dark as well as stuffy.' Those were the words for him.

Howards End, E. M. Forster (1910)

9

Finding information

Whenever you have to write, first think about the subject. Make sure that you understand the title, the question that you must answer, or the terms of reference (see p. 103). Ask the questions recommended on page 42. Get as far as you can, preparing your topic outline, before you look for other sources of information. Otherwise you will find an original approach to the subject more difficult.

Making a start with your topic outline will also help you to recognize gaps in your knowledge. Then you can look for just the information you require (see table 23). But remember that the time you spend on the search for additional information must be carefully related to the total time available for thinking, planning, writing and revising (see Chapter 5).

The following extracts are from an address on reading, delivered at Manchester in 1903, by John Lubbock.

No one can read a good and interesting book for an hour without being better for it; happier and better, not merely for the moment, but the memory remains . . .

It is indeed most important that those who use a library should use it wisely. Do we make the most of our opportunities? It is a great mistake to imagine that every one knows how to read. On the contrary, I should say that few do so. Two things have to be considered: how to read and what to read.

What to read

Learn to use the author and subject catalogues in your school or college library; and look to see what kinds of books are kept in the reference section of the library. Also use nearby town or city libraries.
In any library, if you have difficulty in finding information on any subject ask a librarian for help. The librarian can also show you how to reserve a book that has been borrowed by another reader, or how to obtain a book on inter-library loan. However, if you are not sure what information you are looking for, ask your teacher or tutor for further advice on where to begin your reading.

Dictionaries. Refer to a good dictionary (see p. 143) if you are uncertain of the correct spelling, pronunciation or meaning of any word. Remember also that there are specialized dictionaries of, for example, the technical terms used in your subjects. And there are dictionaries of abbreviations (see p. 63) and of idiomatic expressions (see table 18, p. 69).

Encyclopaedias are a good starting point for anyone coming new to a subject. The best known, most authoritative and most detailed encyclopaedias in the English Language include the *Encyclopaedia Britannica* and *Chambers' Encyclopaedia.*

Table 23   *Some sources of information*

Activities	Sources
thinking	personal observation
	private records
talking	asking questions
	unpublished records
writing	correspondence
reading	dictionaries
	encyclopedias
	handbooks and standards
	directories
	books
	journals and magazines
	newspapers
	photographs
	maps
	sound recordings
	films

Entries in an encyclopaedia are in alphabetical order. Each entry is written by an expert on the subject. Information and ideas are presented clearly and concisely in a logical order. Always look at the index as well as the entry; this may lead you to other relevant entries.

Handbooks are concise reference books for day-to-day use (see further reading: Appendix 4, p. 141). Each handbook provides information on one subject.

Directories provide names and addresses and sometimes other information. The best known are the telephone directories; but there are other directories of the names of trades, industries and organizations. You should know of such lists of authors and titles as *Books in Print* (published in the United States) and *British Books in Print* (published in Britain). In these you can see whether or not a book that you require is in print; or whether or not the copy you have is the latest edition (see p. 98).

Books. If you wish to know which books are available on any subject, first look at the subject index in your library. Then, to find which books are in the library, consult the appropriate classification numbers in the subject

Lost in words

The time spent in the search for information must be carefully related to the total time available for the work.

catalogue. Here you should find one entry for each book. The book number in this entry indicates where the book, with the same number, is to be found on the shelves.

The easiest way to find if a particular book is in your library is to use the alphabetical catalogue. Most books are listed according to the name of the author or editor, but some are listed by the name of the organization, government department or society which produced the book. Each entry in this catalogue includes, in addition to this name, details of the book and the book number.

This same number, printed on the spine of the book, enables you to find the book on the shelves and enables the librarian to return the book to the same place. In most libraries books are classified according to the Dewey Decimal System (table 24); but many libraries in the United States of America use the Library of Congress System (table 24). Another system, the Universal Decimal System (table 24), is a modified form of Dewey which is used in many libraries of science and technology. This may prove more satisfactory for computer-based information retrieval systems.

Table 24   *Three systems used for classifying books in libraries*

The ten classes of the Dewey Decimal System	*Universal Decimal System*	*Library of Congress System*
000 General works	0	A
Reference books (030)	03	AE
100 Philosophy	1	B
Psychology (150)	15	BF
200 Religion	2	BL
300 Social sciences	3	H
400 Languages	4	P
500 Pure sciences	5	Q
600 Applied sciences	6	
700 The Arts	7	N
800 Literature	8	P
900 Geography (910)	91	G
Biography (920)	92	CT
History (930)	93	C

In the Dewey Decimal System there are ten classes (numbered 000 to 900 in table 24). Within each of these classes there are nine divisions (for example, 910, 920 and 930 in table 24). Books are further classified within each division; and the full number of each book (the book number) is printed on its spine.

The librarian would like to put all books on one subject together on the shelves but this is not possible. Some books on fungi, for example, are classified with other books on botany, and others with books on agriculture, medicine, brewing, timber decay, stored products, etc. The librarian may also have difficulty in classifying interdisciplinary books. So if you want to know which books are in the library, you must use the author and subject catalogues.

Magazines and journals. Current issues of magazines and journals are usually kept together, separate from the books, in the reference section of a library, and back numbers are kept in a store to which readers may not have direct access.

No library can afford to buy all the thousands of magazines and journals (periodicals) published each year. Consult the periodicals catalogue (an alphabetical list in your library) to see which periodicals are purchased regularly.

In magazines and journals, original articles and up-to-date reviews are published. Your teachers are in the best position to say which periodicals are likely to be of most use to you, so that you can look regularly at current issues to see if any articles are of interest.

Students who need recent references should, if they need help, tell the librarian what they wish to know and ask for his or her advice on where to find appropriate abstracting or indexing journals. *Abstracts* include only authors' names and the titles and summaries of articles published in selected periodicals. *Indexing journals* include only lists of authors' names and key words from selected periodicals, which enable you to find articles by particular authors or articles dealing with particular subjects. Remember also that many journals publish an annual index.

Other sources of information. Consider other possible sources of information and ideas, such as maps and photographs, recorded tapes and slides, videotapes and films. These may be kept in a visual aids section of your library; or they may be available in map rooms or other class rooms.

How to read

When you open a book, first look at the date of publication, printed on the reverse of the title page. Look also to see when the book was reprinted or revised. Minor corrections may be made when a book is reprinted but a new edition normally indicates an extensive revision. Always consider how up-to-date the work is before you read further: you will have to refer to other books, as well or instead, if you require more recent information and ideas.

When you have decided what to read, remember that an effort is required of the reader as well as of the writer. Read carefully to make sure that you take the intended meaning. Read critically as a stimulus to thinking. If possible, obtain information from more than one source. This will help you to see the subject from more than one point of view.

However, remember that what you read is not necessarily true. You may read to get the facts of the matter but the more you read the more you find that the experts disagree. Read critically, therefore: consider the evidence and arguments presented and try to distinguish facts from opinions.

Read with a purpose to see how other people organize and present their thoughts, or to get background information and ideas, or in search of information on specific points. You do not need to read the whole of every book or article that you consult. Some books are written as reference books but even those that can be read as a whole may also be read in part. Look at the preface to see the author's intentions, and use the contents pages and the index. Get into the habit of skim reading to find just the information that you need at the time. This is a good way to start reading about a subject, because you will remember best those things that interest you most.

Making notes as you read

Do not waste time copying long passages from your textbooks or making detailed notes. If you do this as a habit, consider whether or not your time could be better spent. Also, remember that if your notes are voluminous they may be too long for use in revision for examinations.

Buy up-to-date textbooks on each aspect of your course and then learn in two ways: by reading the relevant parts of each book several times; and by preparing concise notes. Include page references in your notes so that you can consult relevant passages in textbooks easily when you need them.

Unless you intend to read the whole of any book, decide what information you require and then go immediately to relevant pages.

Write concise notes with numbered headings and supporting details marked by letters. Use capitals for important words; use arrows to indicate connections; and use tables and diagrams to summarize information and ideas.

Concise notes are an aid to study. Note-taking helps you to concentrate – because you have to decide which paragraphs are relevant to your immediate needs. It is best to read a passage and then to make concise notes, in your own words, as you read it again.

Your notes should be similar to the author's topic outline and they are likely to be of most use when you are preparing a topic outline for a composition of your own (see p. 42). Each heading in your notes may then remind you of the topic for a paragraph, and the sub-headings and key words should remind you of supporting details, as you exercise judgement in deciding what to include and how to arrange your thoughts.

Good concise notes made as you read are also an aid to revision. It is best if they can be brief notes added to or combined with your lecture notes (fig. 6), so that you have one set of notes on each subject. Indeed,

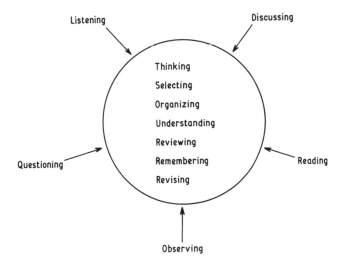

Fig. 6 *The central place of your notes in active study. The different ways in which making notes contributes to learning are included in the circle. The arrows indicate additions to your notes and to your knowledge and understanding, from different sources.*

when you feel that you have a good grasp of any subject you should consider making even more concise notes. If you prepare such *notes of your notes* on index cards, with one card for each subject or topic, these will be most useful when you revise for examinations.

Keep a note of everything you read. As a heading, note the author's name and initials and the date of the latest edition of the book. Then note the title, the name of the publisher and the place of publication. For an article, note the author's name and initials, the date of publication, the title of the article, the name of the magazine or journal, the volume number, the part number and the page numbers covered by the article. You will need such complete bibliographic details if you wish to consult the same work again or refer someone else to the same source of information. In your notes always note the pages from which each note is taken.

Improve your writing

1 *Using your notes*. When you have to answer a question, do not refer to your notes until you have prepared a first draft of your topic outline (see p. 42). This will help you to produce an original answer. You can then revise your topic outline as you consult your notes and refer to books; but when you write, do not copy complete sentences unless you acknowledge their source (see p. 108). Do not copy long passages from books; if you do your answer will not be your own and the different styles of writing will be apparent. It is better to summarize information and ideas and, if appropriate, to acknowledge their source and to provide a list of sources of information at the end of your composition (see above).

2 *Organizing your studies*. To make good use of your study time:
   (a) consider what you have to do;
   (b) set yourself short-term and long-term objectives;
   (c) establish an order of priorities;
   (d) concentrate first on the essentials; and
   (e) organize your work. In one evening's work you may make most progress if you do not work for three hours at one task but for one hour each at three different tasks.

Effective study involves acquiring knowledge, understanding your work, and organizing your knowledge and ideas. In course work and examinations you have the opportunity to display your knowledge and understanding, in writing, in an organized way which is the result of your thinking.

3 *Storing information.* You do not have to remember everything that you write but you do need a convenient system for classifying and storing information so that you have immediate access to all your written work. You can use paper clips to hold A4 sheets together and you can file your work on a particular subject in an A4 envelope. Then keep the envelopes in order in a cardboard box (e.g. a cereal packet); and keep index cards in order in a cardboard box (e.g. a shoe box). More expensive hardcover files, box files and filing drawers are not necessary.

10

Writing an extended essay or a project report

In many courses at school and college you may have the opportunity to work on your own – but with a supervisor to guide you. In such project work you gather information either by reading or by a combination of reading and practical work, and then present your findings as an extended essay or project report. Preparing this report is a test of your ability: (1) to show your knowledge of the subject; (2) to communicate information and ideas in writing, supported if appropriate by tables and illustrations; and (3) to complete the work in a given time.

Many students make the mistake of completing their project work and then preparing their project report. You are advised to read this chapter, therefore, before starting the work upon which your extended essay or project report will be based.

Choosing a subject

Your supervisor will help you to define the purpose and scope of the project so that you know exactly what is required, and to try to ensure that all that has to be done (see p. 106) can be fitted into the time available. You will have to complete this work in a limited number of weeks; and during this time you cannot afford to neglect other work.

Before starting, make sure that any essential equipment or materials will be available when you need them. Check that the essential sources of information for your project are available in your library or can be obtained from elsewhere.

If possible, look at satisfactory reports completed by other students (in previous years) to get an idea of what they have been able to do in the time available. Choose a subject in which you are already interested and which will complement and support your other studies.

Do not attempt too much. Your extended essay or project report will have a concise title, but this should be followed by a clear statement of your *terms of reference*. At school or college, in set work and in examinations, you have to answer questions. Each question must be clearly worded so that you know exactly what is required in your answer. Similarly, in business or industry, any report is preceded by clearly worded terms of reference. These tell you what is required. They may be written by your supervisor or, if the project is your own idea, you may write your own terms of reference and then have them approved by your supervisor before you start work on the project.

Assessing extended essays and projects

An extended essay or project may provide an opportunity for you to display initiative, ingenuity and originality; and an opportunity for you to demonstrate your ability to select relevant material and present this in a way that is appropriate for the intended audience. Your extended essay or project report should therefore indicate, as appropriate, not only what you have done but also your approach to the problems involved, to the interpretation of work done by others, and to the analysis and interpretation of any new observations. Because of all these things, as in all other course work, what you write and how you write will play a major part in the assessment of your work.

It is difficult for an examiner to arrive at an objective assessment of project work: this is particularly true for an external examiner who has not been in any way associated with the work. Unless there is an oral examination, the extended essay or project report is the external examiner's only guide to the quality of the project work.

It may be difficult for any examiner to decide how much of the report is the student's own work and how much is the supervisor's. All students need help with the choice of subject (see p. 102). The supervisor should then provide a title or clear terms of reference, in writing, and should try to ensure that the work begins well.

Different projects involve different methods of investigation: some are based on published work, some include the results of interviews, and some provide more scope than others for the student to show initiative, ingenuity and originality. These differences, which make objective assessment difficult, must be carefully considered if all students are to be treated fairly.

There is probably no one correct solution to these problems but it is possible to list things which should influence the final assessment. These cannot all be judged at the end of the work.

1 The student's approach to the project: his ability to define clearly the problem to be tackled or the purpose of the work, if the subject was chosen by the student.
2 The thoroughness with which the project work was tackled in relation to the time available, and the logical planning of the work.
3 The accuracy with which information is recorded.
4 The student's ability to interpret work by others, to make personal observations, or to analyse numerical data (as appropriate) and to draw conclusions.
5 The student's ability to relate his own work to his knowledge of the subject derived from the work of others.
6 The student's ability to select relevant material and to reject what is irrelevant, and to present a clear, concise and well-organized written report.

These aspects of the work might be considered of comparable importance and given equal weight in a marking scheme. But whatever method of assessment is adopted, each student should be told, before the project is started, how the extended essay or project report is to be presented and how the project as a whole will be assessed.

Preparing an extended essay or project report

Arrangement

Different kinds of work will be reported in different ways. To encourage uniformity, which makes marking easier, notes for guidance will normally be issued to students taking a particular course. For example, see p. 110.

A project which is based upon a literature search and reading, with no supporting personal observations, will be written as an extended essay or review. As in any other essay, you will include an introduction and a conclusion but the body of the essay will comprise many paragraphs. These must be arranged in a logical order and you will help yourself and your readers if you group closely related paragraphs below appropriate headings and sub-headings. You must therefore plan your report, just as you would plan any other composition.

If a project involves the collection and analysis of data, as well as the study of relevant published work, the project report may be arranged as in table 25.

Using the accepted headings, and knowing the kind of information placed by convention below each heading, makes writing easier and helps readers to find answers to their questions: Who? When? Where? Why? How? What?

Table 25 *The parts of a project report*

Part	Content
Cover sheet	Full title of project. Your name. Name of course of study of which the project is part. Name of school or college. Date.
Title page	Full title of project. Your name.
Acknowledgements	Who helped?
List of contents	Headings and main sub-headings used in report.
Introduction	Why did you do the work? What was the problem? If a literature survey is required, include a sub-heading as part of your introduction.
Methods	How did you do it?
Results	What did you find?
Discussion	What do you make of your results? How do they compare with those of others?
Conclusions	What do you conclude? Are you able to answer any of the questions raised in your *Introduction*?
Summary	What are your main findings?
Sources of information	Give full bibliographic details (see p. 100) for every publication cited in your report.
Appendices	Include, for example, tables of data collected in your investigations and summarized in your *Results*.

Another type of project, preparing an instruction manual, may be appropriate in some courses. See the advice on preparing instructions (Chapter 4). The project report may then be arranged as follows: Cover;

Title page; Acknowledgements; List of contents; Description of equipment; Operating instructions; Maintenance instructions; Servicing instructions; Fault-finding and fault-correction.

In other courses, a suitable project might be the preparation of a guide to the organization and work of an agency, institution, firm or service. Such a project report might be arranged as follows: Cover; Title page; Acknowledgements; List of contents; Introduction (including the reasons for the existence of the agency, institution, etc., and the purpose of the project report); Method of enquiry (including how you obtained the information presented in your report, and what problems you encountered); Results (of your enquiry); Conclusions; Summary; Sources of information; Appendices.

Whatever the nature of your project, you will work on it for several weeks and the written account of your work will probably be longer and more demanding than anything you have written previously. It must be carefully planned so that each aspect of your work can be reported in the most appropriate place. Consider the suggestions on arrangement in this chapter, but do not be bound by conventions if you have some good reason for preferring a different arrangement or new headings.

Decide how to arrange your essay or report after you have discussed your ideas with your supervisor and read the relevant parts of any syllabus, regulations or notes for guidance issued by the examiners.

Writing

Do not complete your investigations or literature search and then start to write, and do not spend so much time on these things that you have no time to write. On the contrary, as soon as you have agreed on the title and scope of the work with your supervisor, try to allocate your time to thinking and planning, to the search for information or to collecting and analysing data, and to writing and revising. Remember that you will need time for preparing diagrams. If the report is to be typed you must also leave time for this.

When you are writing an extended essay or project report, imagine that you are writing not only for your supervisor but also for an examiner, whose precise interests you will not know. If you are preparing an instruction manual, make sure that it can be understood by the kind of person who is most likely to use the equipment. Whatever you are writing, first try to identify your readers and then keep their needs in mind.

Start writing as soon as you have decided what your project is to be about. Writing a first draft of the Introduction will concentrate your attention on the purpose of your project and its relationship to other people's work. This should help you to see your limited objective in a wider perspective.

Write the Methods section as soon as you have decided how you will do the work. And then write an account of each part of your investigation as soon as it is complete – so that, if necessary, you can easily check your work.

Projects are assessed not weighed

Do not attempt too much; you must complete the project in the time available and you should not neglect your other studies.

Tables (see p. 81) and illustrations (see p. 32) to be included in the Methods, Results or Discussion sections of the report should be prepared as your work proceeds. There should be only one table or illustration on each page, unless you wish to facilitate comparison. And the size of each table or illustration should be decided so that, if possible, it fits upright on the page.

Ensure that there is at least one reference to each table and illustration in the text, but do not repeat information in the text if it is presented in either a table or illustration. Similarly, do not repeat information in an illustration that is given in a table. Decide how to present information and then present it once.

Make notes of points that you expect to include in your Discussion, as they come to mind. Then, when the work is complete, you can write the Discussion and revise the other parts of your report.

Read Chapter 5 again: 'Writing and thinking'. To make your work easier, write each heading and sub-heading, and even each paragraph, on a separate sheet of paper; and prepare each table and diagram on a separate sheet. This will help you to ensure that each paragraph deals with only one topic, or with very closely related topics. It will help you to keep information on each aspect of your work in the right place, to avoid repetition, and to incorporate new material or revise the order of presentation. Unwanted material can be easily removed. In this way, while you are working, your draft remains a concise and up-to-date progress report.

Do not extract paragraphs or even sentences from works by other people and then present them as your own. Instead, bring together information and ideas, including summaries made in the course of your reading. These should be acknowledged. You may do this by inserting numbers in parenthesis in your composition, corresponding to the numbers used in your list of Sources of Information. Alternatively, you may give the author's name in your composition (followed immediately by the date of publication of the work in parenthesis) and then give full bibliographical details in the list of sources (as explained on p. 100). If you do not receive clear instructions from your supervisor, you will need either to ask his or her advice on the method of citation to be used or to look at satisfactory project reports or extended essays completed by students in previous years of the same course.

Improve your writing

Checking an extended essay or project report

You cannot check the completed report properly by reading it through once or twice. It is necessary to check one thing at a time.

1 Are the cover and title pages complete? Do they provide all the information required by your examiners?
2 Does the title provide the best concise description of the contents of the report?

3 Do you need a contents page? If so, make sure that the headings and sub-headings are identical with those used in the report.
4 Does each part of the report start with a main heading at the top of a page?
5 Are the purpose and scope of your project (or your terms of reference) stated clearly and concisely in the Introduction? Is everything included in the report relevant to the title? Do you keep within the scope of the project as stated in your Introduction; or do you comply with your terms of reference?
6 Has anything essential been left out? Are all your readers' questions answered (see p. 105)? Are your conclusions clearly expressed?
7 Is each paragraph necessary? Is it in the best place? Is the connection between paragraphs clear?
8 Is the report well balanced? Have you given too much attention to details and neglected essential points (see Emphasis, p. 83)? Is there any important point which could be more clearly expressed? Is anything original emphasized sufficiently?
9 Is each statement accurate, based on sufficient evidence, free from contradictions, and free from errors of omission? Are there any words, such as many or few, which should be replaced by numbers?
10 Are there any mistakes in spelling or grammar?
11 Could the meaning of any sentence be better expressed? Is each sentence easy to read? Does it sound well when read aloud?
12 Are any technical terms, symbols or abbreviations sufficiently explained?
13 Are all the sources of information listed correctly (see p. 100)? The list should include all the references mentioned in the text *but no others*.
14 Are all figures, tables, and pages numbered and in order?
15 Does the revised report look neat and does it read well?

When you have completed, checked and corrected your first draft, your supervisor may like to read it and make suggestions for its improvement. Otherwise, ask someone else to read your work. They may be able to point out inconsistencies or mistakes, sentences and paragraphs that are not relevant or are out of place, and parts that are ambiguous or difficult to understand. You should consider these comments and then make any necessary additions, deletions or corrections. You may need to rewrite the report before you hand it in (or have it typed). Even if the report is to be typed, you must ensure that it is legible and neatly set out for the typist and that any instructions about arrangement and presentation are clearly stated.

Presentation

1 Use A4 paper; and for a hand-written report use wide-lined paper.
2 Include separate cover and title pages; and a list of contents.
3 Start each main heading at the top of a new page. Centre main headings but not sub-headings.
4 For a hand-written report leave a 25-mm ruled margin on the left-hand side of the page and leave a similar space at the right-hand side. For a typed report leave a 40-mm margin on the left and 25-mm on the right and at the top and bottom of the page.
5 A typed report should be presented in double spacing on one side of the page only.
6 Number all pages, except the cover, title and contents pages, in the top right-hand corner of each page.
7 Keep a copy.

11

Doing your best in examinations

Preparation

Only you can decide how you should prepare for a written examination; but consider the following suggestions.

If possible, obtain a copy of the syllabus early in your course so that you can get a good idea of what you will be studying. However, your best guide to what will be expected in examinations should be your lecture notes, your set work, and past examination papers.

Work steadily throughout your course and keep up to date with all set work. Those who hand in work late create a poor impression of themselves; and those who always hand in work on time are most likely to be in control of their studies.

Make sure that you understand all aspects of your work as you go along, and that you have a good set of notes (see pages 8 and 98).

Obtain recent past question papers so that you can see how the papers are arranged, what choice of questions is given in each subject, and what kinds of questions are asked. Plan answers to the kinds of questions that are likely to be set in your examinations. If you are uncertain of the precise meaning of any question, or exactly what is required in the answer, discuss this with a teacher. Planning answers will help you to concentrate on your studies and will give direction to your work.

Prepare a time-table for your revision (see also p. 6) and start revising six to eight weeks before your examinations. Remember that in revising you should be simply refreshing your memory. That is to say, you should not be learning things for the first time.

Revise each subject over the whole revision period, not one subject at a time. Work on your notes of your notes (see p. 99) and revise all parts of your work so that it does not matter too much if some of your favourite topics are not examined.

Some people like to work on the evening before an examination. Others find it best to try to put their work on one side and to relax.

Check the date, time and location of each examination. Get enough sleep in the weeks before your examinations and especially on the night before each examination. Make arrangements to ensure that you wake on time.

Why many students do not get as many marks as they could

The following comments are based on the reports of examiners on advanced school examinations taken by eighteen-year-old students. They apply equally to students in further and higher education.

Use of out-of-date books. Students cannot expect to get a modern approach to their subject from a textbook written twenty years ago.

Poor allocation of time. Because they do not read the instructions at the head of the examination paper, some candidates answer too few questions, some answer too many, and some do not select questions as directed.

Because they do not discipline themselves to organize their time effectively, many candidates spend too much time on some questions and too little on others – as they run out of time. As a result, they may get good marks for some questions but very few for others, with the result that their final mark is not a true reflection of their ability.

Similarly, candidates lose marks if they do not organize their time effectively within each answer. In most answers it is necessary to exercise judgement in deciding how much time to devote to each part of the answer. But in a structured question the allocation of marks may be given in the margin and this is an indication of how much time should be allocated to each part of the answer.

Lack of care in selecting questions when there is a choice. Candidates must read all questions carefully, to make sure that they understand what is required in each answer, before they decide which questions they can best answer. Otherwise they may find, after leaving the examination room, that they have not made a sensible choice.

Lack of thought before starting an answer. Either because they do not read the question carefully or because they do not think carefully enough about what is required, many candidates write long and painstaking answers but are given very few marks – simply because they include much irrelevant material and do not do precisely what is asked of them. The candidate who thinks, selects relevant material, and plans a concise answer to the question set will get many more marks than the candidate who writes at greater length – who reproduces dictated notes or is determined to write *all he knows* about the subject in the hope that the examiner will look for anything that happens to be relevant and delete everything that is irrelevant. In practice, examiners do not waste their time on doing things which the candidates should do for themselves. Quality, completeness and relevance are required – not quantity for its own sake.

Answering a similar question, perhaps one set in a previous year, instead of the question set. Many candidates, having carefully prepared an answer before entering the examination room – as part of their revision – seem to be incapable of readjusting. They are not prepared to reorganize their knowledge of the subject so that they can present a considered answer to the question set.

Giving an incomplete answer. Some candidates do not answer part of the question because they either do not plan their answer or do not work to their topic outline.

Other candidates obviously have planned their answer but they omit evidence or examples, or omit other relevant material – perhaps because they think it is too elementary. It is best to include all relevant aspects of an answer to the question asked, even if some introductory material is mentioned only briefly and in passing. Otherwise, the examiner must assume that you are ignorant of some parts of the answer.

Failure to make clear one's understanding of the material presented. Marks are given not simply for relevant material, well ordered and clearly presented, but also for understanding.

The candidate must show that he understands why all parts of his answer are relevant to the question set. For example, words from the question may be used at appropriate points in the answer to draw attention to the relevance of what is being presented.

Poor presentation. Candidates should consider the examiner, who has many papers to mark, and should take a pride in the way they present their work. They should start by indicating clearly the number of the question being answered; and should make sure that their writing is legible. A careless scrawl makes an unfavourable impression from the start – and examiners can give marks only for what they can read.

Candidates should not leave gaps, for example at the bottom of a page, and then continue the answer on a later page. Otherwise the examiner may give a mark and then find, on turning the page, that the answer is continued and that the mark already given must be reconsidered.

Inadequate vocabulary. Many candidates are frustrated because they cannot find the words to express their thoughts precisely and completely.

Any examinee should try to avoid clichés, colloquial expressions and slang, which are all signs of an inadequate vocabulary.

Poor spelling. Spelling words incorrectly always creates an unfavourable impression, and it can result in misunderstandings.

Poor punctuation and grammar. Some candidates do not understand even the simpler rules of punctuation. Because of errors in punctuation and grammar such candidates write ambiguous sentences. But examiners can mark only what is written – not what they think the candidate probably meant.

Technique

Most of the faults listed on pages 112 to 114 can be summed up in three words: poor examination technique.

The following advice can be understood by a student working alone, but may also be used by teachers in class discussions both before and after a test or examination.

If possible, examination scripts should be returned to students so that they can see their mistakes and appreciate where they have failed to express themselves clearly.

How examination papers are set and marked

Consider how examination papers are marked so that in planning each answer you can try to score maximum marks. Learn to see each part of any answer, and each paragraph, as an opportunity to gain marks by adding *relevant* information and ideas, and by showing your understanding.

1 In most examinations marks are divided equally between the questions to be answered so that there are 25 marks per question when four questions are to be answered, and 20 marks per question when five are to be answered. You must, therefore, answer the right number of questions.

2 To be fair to all candidates, examiners allocate the marks which may

be obtained for each question according to a marking scheme. This is a topic outline, similar to the one that you will prepare before you start your answer (unless only a short answer is needed).

If a question is set in parts, a certain number of marks will be allocated for each part of the answer. However, whether or not the question is set in parts, the examiner will expect you to refer to, and to show your understanding of, all those things which are relevant to the answer.

If you do not answer all parts of a question or if you give an answer that is otherwise incomplete, you cannot score full marks on that question.

Making the best use of your time in an examination

1 Read and obey all the instructions at the top of the first page of the question paper. Make sure that you know how much time you are allowed and how many questions you must answer. Look to see if there are any compulsory questions, or any restrictions on your choice of questions.

2 If you have a choice of questions read them all carefully to make sure that you understand what is required in each answer. Then select the questions which you can answer most fully. Otherwise you may realize, after leaving the examination, that you could have answered another selection of questions and obtained better marks.

3 Allocate your time so that you can answer the right number of questions. The instructions at the head of the paper may give guidance about how much time you should spend on the parts of a paper. If the number of marks allocated to a question (or to the parts of a question) is stated in the right-hand margin of the question paper or at the end of the question, this should help you to allocate your time.

If all questions carry the same number of marks, divide your time equally between the questions. Do not spend more time on those questions that you know most about. Remember that it is easier to score half marks on a question that you do not know much about than it is to score full marks when you think you can write a good answer. The first few marks are the easiest to obtain, with a little thought, if you know anything about the subject. But a little extra time spent on a question, upon which you have already spent long enough, is likely to be less rewarding.

4 Keep an eye on the time. Allow a proportion of the time available for reading all the questions at the beginning, for planning your

answers, and for reading through your work at the end to correct any slips of the pen and to add any important points that you did not remember the first time through.

5 If in spite of planning you find that you are running out of time, it is better to answer your last question in note form than to leave it unanswered. In a written examination you will be given some marks for a good topic outline.

6 Do not waste time. Arrive at the examination before the start but try to relax: do not talk to others about the examination while you are waiting to enter the room. Use your time effectively during the examination. Do not leave before the end.

Answering questions in an examination

An examination is a test not only of your knowledge of the subject but also of your ability to understand the questions and to organize your knowledge in effective answers.

1 Read the question carefully to make sure that you understand what the examiner wants to know. Answer the question that you have been asked and *not a similar question which you were hoping for*.

2 If the examination comprises essay-type questions, you may find it best to plan all your answers quickly at the beginning of the examination – so that you can reconsider each topic outline immediately before you start to write each answer.

3 Mark the number of the question clearly in the left-hand margin of your answer book.

4 In an examination you cannot spend much time on thinking about how to begin. However, in your first paragraph you will probably use some words or phrases from the question in a context which makes clear to the examiner that you do understand the question. Indeed, the first sentence or paragraph, if appropriate, should give the essence of your answer.

5 Get to the point quickly and keep to the point. Plan your answer so that it is well organized and well balanced, and so that you can say all that you wish to say without digression or repetition in the time available. By distinct paragraph breaks and, if appropriate, by concise sub-headings, make clear to the examiner where one aspect of the question has been dealt with and the next begins.

6 Do not make vague statements. Give reasons and examples. Include enough explanation. Do not leave things out because you think they are too simple or too obvious. Do not include anything

that is irrelevant but make sure that everything relevant is included, however briefly, to show your knowledge and understanding. Your answer must be complete, because the examiner cannot assume that you know anything, and can give marks only for what you write.

7 If you include anything that is not obviously relevant, explain why it is relevant. An examination is not simply a test of your ability to recall facts and ideas. It also provides an opportunity to show your ability to distinguish relevant from irrelevant material.

8 If you are asked to discuss then you must discuss all sides of the question and refer to any unsolved problems.

9 If you are asked to compare you should also refer to any differences, even if the question does not ask you to compare and contrast. If you are asked to compare two things, do not simply describe one and then the other. In every paragraph, after the introduction, make comparisons and point out differences.

10 If a question is set in several parts it is best to answer each part separately, and if the parts are indicated by letters (a, b, c, etc.) you should use these letters to indicate the parts of your answer. If the parts of a question are not labelled by letters, you should use appropriate sub-headings to draw attention to the parts of your answer that relate to each part of the question.

11 If a question is set in several parts, you must spend enough time on each part of your answer. Unless you have some very good reason for not doing so, you should answer the parts in the order in which they are set, because the examiner will expect to mark them in this order.

12 If the number of marks allocated to each part of a question is indicated in the margin (next to the question), this should indicate not only how much time you should devote to each part of your answer but also how many relevant points may be needed for an adequate answer to each part.

13 Make sure that any diagram is simple so that you can complete it quickly and neatly. Use coloured pencils, if necessary, to represent different things, but do not waste time on shading.

Each diagram should be in the most appropriate place but should be numbered· so that you can refer to it in other parts of your answer. If diagrams are necessary they should complement your writing – making explanation easier and enabling you to present information and ideas that could not be adequately presented in words alone. Effective diagrams should therefore reduce the number of words needed in the text. Do not waste time conveying the same information both in words and in a diagram.

14 Make sure that your writing is legible and use black or blue-black ink. Do not write with a coloured pen or pencil because, if you do, your writing may be mistaken for the examiner's corrections.

    When you have completed a question, it is a good idea to put a sloping line through your plan (rough work) so that the examiner can see at once that this is not part of your answer.

Do not waste time on shading

In examinations use all your time effectively.

Improve your writing

1 Work to a time-table throughout your course of study (see p. 6), and revise all aspects of your work regularly. For example, at the weekend you may review aspects of the previous week's work, and in vacations, you should revise the previous term's or year's work as well as looking forward to the term or year ahead. It is not possible to revise everything in the few weeks preceding an examination unless you have understood, learned and revised throughout the course.

2 Try not only to keep abreast of your work but also to master your

subject. Teachers find that they learn most when they have to teach their subject. In preparing topic outlines it may help if you think about what you would say if you had to teach this aspect of your subject, and if you consider the kinds of questions that your students might ask.

Also, to maintain and develop your interest in the course, consider your studies in a wider perspective. For example, try to obtain relevant vacation employment.

3 List the questions set on each topic in recent examinations (for example, in the last two years). Incorporate these lists in the relevant parts of your notes, followed by the topic outlines prepared as you study and revise.

4 To develop your ability to work under pressure, as in examinations, test yourself regularly by writing answers to questions in the time that will be allowed in an examination. Also, complete some past papers to give yourself practice in finishing the number of questions required in the set time.

Always write on wide-lined paper, which is the kind that is provided in most examinations, and leave a 25-mm margin on the left hand side of each page.

12

Speaking for yourself

Asking questions

When you take notes in a lesson or lecture, note particularly anything that you do not fully understand or any aspect about which you would like further information. You may mark these by a question mark in the margin, so that when the time comes you are ready to ask questions (see table 2, p. 14). Some teachers like to clarify any possible misunderstandings or to answer any relevant questions as they go along; others prefer to wait until the end.

Get into the habit of asking questions. Good questions help to keep everyone attentive and to stimulate thought.

Rewriting notes can be a waste of time (see p. 12). However, read carefully through your notes to make sure that you understand them and that there are no gaps. If necessary look at your textbook or try to find the answers to your questions from other sources of information (see Chapter 9). If any questions remain or if you require further information, you will be ready to ask questions at the next opportunity.

Answering questions: being interviewed

Before an interview for a place at college or for a job, find out as much as you can about the course or the employer – and about the selection procedures used. This is very important: it is something that could influence the success of your interview – and so the rest of your life. The more you know, the better you will be able to talk about the work that will be expected of you. You will be able to ask sensible questions. Remember that in a short time the interviewers have to decide how interested you are and how enthusiastic, as well as how well qualified. They have to make judgements about your personality.

When you attend an interview, your appearance and attitude are as important as what you say. You are most likely to be interviewed by middle-aged people who, after years of experience, have reached positions of responsibility. Your dress and language should be appropriate for the occasion. You must not arrive late.

Before the formal interview, if you are given a guided tour of the premises or shown equipment, you may be asked questions and have the opportunity to ask intelligent questions, to display your interest, and so to create a favourable first impression. Learn as much as you can from your conversations and observations.

When the time comes for your interview, walk confidently into the room. Do not sit until you are invited to do so. Sit up so that your clothes look good and so that you feel comfortable, self-confident and alert. Conversation in an interview is likely to be formal and not immediately relaxed; but a good interviewer will help you to feel at ease. He will tell you who he is, and will introduce you to the other people present.

You are likely to be asked, first, for your name. This is to make sure that you are the person expected at this time. You may then be asked to confirm other details given in your application, such as when and where you were born and where you were educated. Answering such factual questions gives you time to relax a little. Speak clearly and use your normal speaking voice. As in normal conversation, look at the person or persons you are addressing and do not be afraid to smile occasionally. Show your interest and enthusiasm.

Listen carefully to the questions and try to give short and straightforward answers to any simple questions. However, do not feel that you have to respond immediately to every question. If you feel that a few moments of thought will help you to give a more complete and sensible answer, allow yourself a little time. Try to summarize your thoughts when a question calls for a longer reply, so that you do not talk for too long at a time. The interviewer can ask further questions if more detail is required.

Note that if you write in your application (see p. 25) or in your *curriculum vitae* (see p. 28) that you have certain interests, you must expect to be asked questions about these subjects. Your answers will indicate the extent of your interest – and how enthusiastic you are. So look through your application when you are preparing for the interview. This should help you to anticipate certain questions and to consider your replies. For example, if you have done project work you may be asked questions about what you did; and if you have had a period of vacation employment or a training year, you are likely to be asked how you feel you benefited from the experience. See also table 26.

Table 26   *Possible sequence of questions and answers at the beginning of an interview*

Possible questions	Possible replies
Good morning Mr Jones, my name is Telford. I am the Product Development Manager	How do you do.
Please sit down.	Thank you.
As you know, we are here today to interview applicants for . . . I would just like to confirm a few details from your application.	
1 I see that you are twenty-one.	That is correct.
You went to school in . . .	Yes.
Note. There will probably be other factual questions (e.g. about the subjects you have studied, and about vacation work or other employment).	
2 I see that you are keen on sport.	Yes sir. I play cricket in my summer vacations for . . . I am a spin bowler.
What is it about cricket that appeals to you?	*Note.* By this time the interviewer has already found out quite a lot about you. Your answer to this open-ended question will tell him much more about your personality.
3 You say in your application that you like reading.	Yes, I read for relaxation.
What kind of books do you prefer?	I read novels mostly.

Who are your favourite
authors?

What is it that you like
about the novels by . . .?

Note. If you have nothing
to say at this stage
the interviewer will conclude
that you are not, after all,
interested in reading.

4 Tell me, Mr Jones, why did
you apply for a place on
this course/vacation work
with us/a training place here/
this vacancy?

Note. This is something
that you should have con-
sidered before preparing your
application. You should therefore be ready with an
intelligent and enthusiastic
reply.

5 What qualities do you feel
you have that make you suited
to this post?

Note. Be prepared for such
a question, which will give
you the opportunity to state,
positively, why you consider
you would make a success
of the job.

Be prepared, during the interview, to take opportunities to draw attention to your interests and experiences which you particularly wish the interviewer or the interviewing committee to know about. Volunteer such information at appropriate points, but try not to give the impression that you are boasting or that you are conducting the interview.

Towards the end of the interview you will almost certainly be asked if you have any questions. Be prepared for this. Think before the interview and, if necessary, make a note of one or two questions that you would particularly like to ask. If you are seeking employment, the starting salary will probably already have been made clear but you may wish to ask about training opportunities and promotion prospects.

Do not hesitate to speak if you find that the chairman is closing the interview without asking if there is anything you wish to say or any questions you wish to ask. He may just not care whether or not you have any questions, or he may have forgotten to ask: in either case you have nothing to lose.

Taking part in a tutorial

In a tutorial you may have the opportunity to discuss with a tutor, and perhaps with a few students, your plan for an essay or your thoughts expressed in a completed essay. At least, you should know in advance what subject is to be discussed. You should then prepare for the tutorial.

Given a title, you can prepare a plan – similar to a topic outline for an essay. In this your thoughts on the subject are organized, so that in the tutorial you will have something to say. Then leave plenty of space in your plan so that you can add relevant ideas contributed by others. Listen carefully; then make your comments brief but to the point. Ask for clarification. Ask other questions. Criticize and comment. If you use tutorials and other discussion groups in this way, you will learn both from your preparation and from the discussion.

Preparing for a seminar

If you attend a seminar you will know what subject is to be discussed. You can make preparations, as for a tutorial.

If you are asked to introduce the subject for discussion at a seminar, remember that if the whole seminar is to take thirty minutes your introduction must not take more than ten. Before the seminar, prepare a plan of what you wish to say. Out of ten minutes you may spend two on introducing the subject. You will then have just enough time to refer briefly to two or three aspects upon which you consider the discussion should be concentrated. Inexperienced speakers usually try to make too many points and to support their arguments with too much detail – with the result that they run out of time.

If you have not given a seminar previously, you will find it helpful to tell someone what you are planning to say. By doing this you will learn, before the seminar, how little you are able to say in the time available.

The best seating plan for a seminar is one in which the participants are in a circle, perhaps around a table. Everyone should make brief notes while other people are talking. Make a note of what is being said and of things you may wish to contribute to the discussion. Because the time for the discussion is short, all questions and answers and comments should be concise.

During the seminar, look at people whenever you are talking. Look around to make sure that everyone is listening, and speak clearly so that they all hear every word.

Giving a talk

Teachers find that they learn most about their subject, and learn quickly and easily, when they have to teach others. Teachers may therefore encourage students to prepare for a tutorial, or to introduce a seminar, or to deliver a short talk: these are effective methods of instruction.

However, even if you do not have the opportunity to give a talk as part of your course work, you may wish to speak at meetings, or to give short talks at clubs, or you may have to talk to a group of people after you have completed your education – for example, as part of an employer's selection procedure which may last several days, or as part of your employment when you may have to give instruction as part of a training course.

Preparing and planning

Consider your audience and ask yourself: What do I wish to achieve in the time available?

1 Make sure that you know enough about the subject. Do any necessary background reading. You must be self-confident if you are to gain the confidence of your audience.

2 Decide on a limited number of main points that you must make. Arrange these in a logical sequence and then check that they are all essential in relation to your aim.

3 You may find it helpful to make a note of each main point on an index card or at the top of a blank sheet of paper – with any essential supporting details or evidence summarized below each heading.

4 The number of main points that can be made in the time available, and the amount of supporting detail required, will depend upon your audience. What prior knowledge, if any, can you assume to be shared by all members of your audience?

5 Consider what visual aids, if any, are required to support your words. For example, decide which words are most important (for example your main headings) and which words may be new to some members of your audience, so that you will remember to write these words on a blackboard or overhead projector.

6 Prepare any necessary stores, equipment or visual aids; and decide exactly when you are going to use them to support your words and to add interest. See visual aids, p. 127.

7 Plan any demonstration that will reinforce your words and add interest.

8 Try to make your talk interesting. This depends upon: (a) your knowledge of the subject and your ability to select what is relevant to this talk; (b) showing that what you have to say is relevant to the needs of this audience – that it follows on from their existing interests or that it will help them in some other way; (c) ensuring variety and simplicity in presentation; (d) letting people see as

well as hear (see visual aids); and (e) avoiding distractions.

9 To make sure that you can finish on time, it is a good idea to go through your talk beforehand, by yourself or with a friend. Remember that you will need to leave time for questions (see delivery, below).

10 Ensure that the room to be used for your talk is the right size and that the equipment you need will be available and in working order.

Delivery

If possible, ensure that the room is warm enough and well ventilated. Try to ensure that no one can see out of a window or hear distracting noises. Stand where everyone can see you but avoid distracting mannerisms such as juggling with chalk, swinging or banging a pointer, or constantly walking to and fro.

1 Speak so that everyone can hear every word. Try not to speak in a monotone. Look around your audience to capture everyone's attention. Maintain eye contact so that you can appreciate the needs of individuals – to see that they do understand. Show your enthusiasm for the subject.

2 If possible, do not read your talk. Use your notes as reminders.

3 Make sure that everyone knows who you are!

4 Say what you are going to talk about. Remind the audience how this follows on from what they already know. Give the reason for your talk. Define your aim. This is your opportunity, in your introduction, to capture attention and promote a desire to listen.

5 In the body of your talk make each of your main points clearly and in a logical order. Pause briefly after each main point has been made, to let everyone know that it is time to start thinking about something else.

6 To ensure that you keep their attention, it is a good idea to give your audience something to do. For example, you may write a word on a blackboard or use some other visual aid to reinforce a main point. They then have something to see as well as something to hear. Or you may ask a question of your audience from time to time – to make them consider something that you want them to consider. Then pause briefly to give everyone time to think before you *either* answer the question yourself *or* invite one person, by name, to attempt an answer.

7 At the end of your talk, summarize each of your main points and state clearly what conclusions you draw. Say why they may be

important for your audience.

8 Leave time for questions. In teaching, questions should be asked at this stage – to enable you to *confirm* that everyone has understood and remembered your main points and your conclusions. Whether or not it is appropriate for you to ask questions, you should always invite questions. Questions from your audience may *reveal misunderstandings*, or may enable you to make *additional relevant points* that you were unable to include in your talk, or may provide a basis for an interesting *discussion*. Therefore, if your talk is for 30 minutes, you may decide to speak for 20 minutes and to leave 10 minutes for questions.

If you are asked a question, repeat the question to make sure that everyone knows exactly what the question is. Then keep your answer short, clear and to the point.

9 *Finish on time.*

Visual aids

Using a blackboard

If you know how to use a blackboard properly, you will be able to prepare effective visual aids quickly at the most appropriate times during your talks.

1 On a green or black board use yellow or white chalk. Remember that only pastel shades will show up on a dark board.
2 Spell any word that may be new to some people in your audience in clear block capitals.
3 Use clear, simple diagrams which can be constructed quickly; you should plan them before your talk.
4 When you turn away from your audience to draw or write, always stop talking.
5 Try not to obscure anyone's view either while you are drawing or afterwards.
6 Give people time to study any diagram quietly, without the distracting effect of your voice.
7 Keep the blackboard clean. Do not allow people to continue looking at what you have finished talking about – once you are trying to interest them in something else.

Using an overhead projector

As with a blackboard, or any other equipment, you will find an overhead projector most useful if you have considered, beforehand, how best to use it.

1 Prefer dark inks on a white screen.
2 Prepare tables and diagrams and then project them before your talk – so that you can check, from the back of the room, that they are all clear and that you have not included too much detail or anything irrelevant.
3 If you write during your talk, make sure that the lines are distinct and that the words are legible. As with a blackboard, spell any word that may be new to some people in your audience.
4 Use a pointer so that you can point at the screen. Do not point at the transparency *with your finger* – this obscures the view.
5 However, you may find it helpful to obscure part of a table or diagram deliberately (with a card) so that you can use just the part that is required at the time.
6 When you write or draw, stop talking. And remember that people may need time to study a table or diagram quietly.
7 Remove each transparency as soon as it has served its purpose.
8 Look at your audience when you speak. Try to make sure that they are looking at what you wish them to see.
9 When you speak, stand away from the projector – next to your notes.

Some tips on talking

1 First get into the habit of asking questions (see p. 120). This will help you to gain confidence. All you have to do is to ask the question, and then listen.
2 In a tutorial agree with your tutor, and with other students, the topics for the paragraphs of an essay. Each topic word or sentence should then be written on a separate index card. The cards should then be shuffled and dealt, upside down, one to each student – as in a card game. Each student in turn is asked to look at his or her card and to speak, without preparation, on the topic for one minute (or longer as the participants become more confident).

Appendix 1
Punctuation

Using punctuation marks to make your meaning clear

If you have difficulty with punctuation you will find it easiest to write short sentences.

A sentence expresses a whole thought. It therefore makes sense by itself. A sentence begins with a capital letter. It includes a verb (see table 27). It ends with a full stop.

Each of these five sentences tells the reader one thing about a sentence, but note that if you write only in short sentences your reader has no sooner started each sentence than he has to stop.

Using punctuation marks to ensure the smooth flow of language

Instead of the five short sentences, the same thoughts could be expressed in two.

A sentence expresses a whole thought: it makes sense by itself. Every sentence starts with a capital letter, includes a verb, and ends with a full stop.

In different sentences you may use the same words to express different thoughts.

Help! You can help. Can you help?

Conversely, in different sentences you may use different words to convey the same thought.

Come! You come. Come here, you!

Table 27   *Parts of speech: classifying words*

Parts of speech	The work words do in a sentence
verbs	Words that indicate action: what is done, or what was done, or what is said to be. The ship *sailed*.
nouns	Names. *Nelson* sailed in this *ship*.
pronouns	Words used instead of nouns so that nouns need not be repeated. *He* sailed in *her*.
adjectives	Words that describe or qualify nouns or pronouns. The *big* ship sailed across the *shallow* sea.
adverbs	Words that modify verbs, adjectives and other adverbs. The big ship sailed *slowly* across the *gently* rolling sea.
prepositions	Each preposition governs, and marks the relation between, a noun or pronoun and some other word in the sentence. The ship sailed *across* the sea *to* America.
conjunctions	Words used to join the parts of a sentence, or to make two sentences into one. The ship went to America *and* came straight back.

Using conjunctions to contribute to the smooth flow of language

Conjunctions (e.g. and, or, but, for, nor, when, which, because) can be used to join parts of a sentence or to make two sentences into one (table 27). They link closely-related thoughts, give continuity to your writing, and help your readers along. However, use each conjunction intelligently and, if possible, not more than once in a sentence.

Remember, also, that some conjunctions must be used in pairs: *both* is always followed by *and*, *either* by *or*, *neither* by *nor*, and *not only* by *but also*.

Using capital letters

Capital initial letters are used for the first word in a sentence, for proper nouns (proper names), for interjections, and for most abbreviations (see p. 64); e.g. His church is St Ann's Church.

For emphasis (see p. 83) a whole word may be written in capitals, but initial capital letters are no longer used for this purpose (see p. 73).

In handwriting a clear distinction should be made between capitals and other letters; and (except possibly in a signature) capitals should not be used as an embellishment.

Punctuation marks that end a sentence

Use no more punctuation marks than are necessary to make your meaning clear. If you find punctuation difficult, begin by mastering the use of the full stop and keep your sentences short and to the point.

Full stop, exclamation mark and question mark

The end of a sentence is indicated by a full stop, exclamation mark or question mark.

You must go. Go! Must you go?

Remember that a question mark is used only after a direct question.

Could you explain, please?
I should appreciate an explanation.
I wonder if I should ask for an explanation.

Punctuation marks used within a sentence

Punctuation marks, used to separate the parts of a sentence, make the reader pause for a shorter time than does a full stop. The more you read and write, the more you will come to appreciate their value.

Comma

Items in a list may be separated by commas, as in the next sentence. To write clear, concise and easily read prose we use commas, semi-colons, colons, dashes, and parentheses. In such a list the comma before the final *and* is essential only if it contributes to clarity.

A comma may also be used to separate the parts (or clauses) in a sentence. The word clause comes from the Latin word *claudere*, to close, and within a sentence commas may be needed to separate (close off) one thought or statement from the next.

A sentence comprising one clause, expressing one thought, is called a simple sentence. It makes one statement.

Each word should contribute to the sentence.
Each sentence should contribute to the paragraph.

> Each paragraph should contribute to the composition.
> Nothing should be superfluous.

However, a sentence may comprise more than one clause – expressing more than one thought. A comma or a conjunction, or both, may then be inserted between the separate statements.

> Each word should contribute to the sentence, each sentence to the paragraph, and each paragraph to the composition. Nothing should be superfluous.

Note that in this example that at the beginning of the second clause the conjunction (and) is understood: there is no need to write it. Similarly, in each clause there is a verb but in the second and third clauses this verb (contribute) is understood.

Use commas to mark separate clauses if they make for easy reading and help you to convey your thoughts. A commenting clause should be enclosed by commas; a defining clause should not be.

> People, who go to church on Sundays, are . . .
> People who go to church on Sundays are . . .

Note the difference in meaning. The first sentence implies that all people go to church on Sundays. The second sentence identifies or defines which people are referred to – those who do go.

Do not add commas at random because you feel that a sentence is too long to be without punctuation marks. Either put the comma in the right place, to convey your meaning, or write the sentence so that your meaning is conveyed clearly without the comma.

> You will be informed, if you send a stamped addressed envelope, after the meeting.

> You will be informed, if you send a stamped addressed envelope after the meeting.

> If you send a stamped addressed envelope you will be informed after the meeting.

Note that the first and third sentences convey the same message; one with commas and the other without.

Dash and parenthesis

Dashes and parentheses (brackets) may be used – in pairs – when an aside is added to a sentence. So if you removed the asides from the last sentence you would be left with a complete sentence: Dashes and parentheses may be used when an aside is added to a sentence. *Parentheses* are used when you wish to insert an example or an explanation. *Dashes* are used to give prominence to an important insertion. But note that the dashes could be replaced by commas, as in this sentence, if you wished to give less prominence to an aside.

One dash may be used if the aside is added at the end of a sentence – as in this sentence.

Colon

Note the use of a colon to introduce either a list (see p. 6) or a quotation (see p. 12). A colon may also be used, in place of a full stop, either (1) between two statements of equal weight (see p. 14), or (2) between two statements if the second is an explanation or elaboration of the first (see p. 41).

Semi-colon

The full stop (or period), the colon, the semi-colon, the dash, the comma, and a pair of parentheses, are called marks, points or stops. They are here placed in order. The full stop gives the longest and most impressive pause. The semi-colon, which gives a longer pause than a comma and a shorter pause than a colon, may contribute to clarity (see pages, 41, 53, 80, 81, and 84).

Other punctuation marks

Apostrophe

First, note that an apostrophe is *never used* in forming the plural: apple becomes apples; criterion, criteria; lady, ladies; man, men; phenomenon, phenomena; and wife, wives.

Then note that if you avoid colloquial English (see p. 68), you will use an apostrophe *or* a possessive adjective *or* a possessive pronoun, only when you wish to indicate that someone or something belongs to someone or something (see p. 138).

Quotation marks

You may use quotation marks when you quote someone's words exactly (see p. 5 and p. 37). However this is not the only way to signpost quotations. For example, in this book extracts are clearly marked in the headings of some tables (see p. 71), or they are marked by indentation (see pp. 88–92). Note that quotation marks are included if they are part of the extract: otherwise they are not used in this book. Many authors now manage without them.

When quoting someone else's work, the part quoted must be complete – including every word and every punctuation mark. Any gaps in the quotation should be indicated by dots (as on p. 4).

The source of each quotation should normally be acknowledged (see p. 4), unless you have some good reason for not doing so (e.g. see p. 38). See also p. 108.

The use of quotation marks to indicate that the word used is not to be understood in its usual sense is to be avoided, because the intended sense may not be clear to the reader. Instead, use words that convey your meaning precisely (see p. 57).

The titles of books, plays and poems should not be marked by quotation marks, as is sometimes recommended, but by underlining (or, in print, by italics, see p. 84). Use underlining to help you to distinguish, for example, between Hamlet (the man) and Hamlet (the title of a play) and between David Copperfield (the name of a character in a book) and David Copperfield (the name of the book).

Improve your writing

The best way to appreciate the usefulness of different punctuation marks is to study one or two pages of any book or article that interests you. Consider why the author has used each punctuation mark. You can repeat this exercise with as many compositions as you choose to study. In writing clear and simple English you can manage without semi-colons and colons, but as you begin to appreciate their value you will want to use them.

Appendix 2
Spelling

You may think, if you spell badly, that spelling does not matter. However, spelling words incorrectly will reduce an educated reader's confidence in your writing. Bad spelling also distracts readers, taking their attention away from the writer's meaning. Good spelling is good manners and is part of efficient communication.

Some reasons for poor spelling

Some words are not spelt as they are pronounced: e.g. answer (anser), gauge (gage), island (iland), mortgage (morgage), psychology (sycology), rough (ruff), sugar (shugar), and tongue (tung). You cannot, therefore, spell all words just as you pronounce them. This is one problem for people who find spelling difficult.

However, those who speak badly are likely to find that incorrect pronunciation does lead to incorrect spelling. In lazy speech secretary becomes secatary; environment, enviroment; police, pleece; computer, compu'er; and so on. If you know that you speak and spell badly, take more care over your speech.

Unfortunately, the speech of teachers and radio or TV announcers does not necessarily provide a reliable guide to pronunciation. Consult a dictionary, therefore, if you are unsure of the pronunciation or spelling of any word. And whenever you have to consult a dictionary to see how a word is spelt, check the pronunciation at the same time. Knowing how to pronounce the word correctly, you may have no further difficulty in spelling it correctly.

If you do not read very much, you give yourself few opportunities for increasing your vocabulary (see Chapter 6) and for seeing words spelt correctly. Reading effective prose (see p. 68) will help you in these and other ways.

Some rules to remember

The best way to improve your spelling is to consult a dictionary and then to memorize the correct spelling of any word that you find you have spelt incorrectly. However, learning the following rules – one at a time – will also help.

1 Remember this rule. When **ie** or **ei** are pronounced **ee**, the **i** comes before the **e** except after **c** (as in believe and receive).
   Notes Seize and species are exceptions to this rule.
      The **ei** is not pronounced **ee** in eight, either, foreign, freight, reign, weight and weir.
2 When words ending in *fer* are made longer, for example when refer is used in making the longer words reference and referred, the *r* is not doubled if, in pronouncing the longer word, you stress the first syllable (as in **ref**erence), but it is doubled if you stress the second syllable (as in re**ferred**).
A *syllable* is a unit of pronunciation which forms a word or part of a word.

	First stress (r)	Second stress (rr)
defer	**def**erence	de**ferred**, de**ferring**
differ	**diff**erence, **diff**ering	
infer	**infer**ence	in**ferred**, in**ferring**
offer	**off**ered, **off**ering	
refer	**refer**ee, **refer**ence	re**ferred**, re**ferring**
suffer	**suff**ering, **suff**erance	
transfer	**transfer**ence	trans**ferred**, trans**ferring**

3 With verbs of more than one syllable, which end with a single vowel (*a, e, i, o* or *u*) followed by a single consonant (a letter that is not a vowel), in forming the past tense or a present or past participle, double the consonant if the last syllable is stressed.

	First stress *(one consonant)*	*Second stress* *(two consonants)*
benefit	benefited, benefiting	
bias	biased	
control		controlled, controlling
excel		excelled, excelling
focus	focused, focusing	
parallel	paralleled	
refer		referred, referring

4 With verbs of one syllable, which end with a single vowel followed by a single consonant, double the consonant before adding *ing*.

run	running
sag	sagging
swim	swimming
whip	whipping

On the other hand, if a verb of one syllable does not end in a single vowel followed by a single consonant, simply add *ing*.

daub	daubing
deal	dealing
feel	feeling
help	helping
sink	sinking
watch	watching

5 When verbs ending in *e* are made into words ending in *ing*, the *e* is lost.

bite	biting
come	coming
make	making
trouble	troubling
write	writing

Exceptions

singe	singeing (to keep the soft g)
agree	agreeing (to keep the ee sound)
flee	fleeing (to keep the ee sound)
hoe	hoeing
dye (colour)	dyeing

With some verbs *ie* is replaced by *y*

die	dying
lie	lying

6 If an adjective (see table 27) ends in *l*, the corresponding adverb (which answers the question: How?) ends in *lly*.

adjective	*adverb*
beautiful	beautifully
faithful	faithfully
hopeful	hopefully
peaceful	peacefully
spiteful	spitefully

7 Some adjectives that end in *y* have corresponding adverbs and nouns and in which the *y* is replaced by an *i*.

adjective	*adverb*	*noun*
busy	busily	business
merry	merrily	merriment

Many people have difficulty in spelling some words correctly because they are unable to distinguish, for example, between there and their, it's and its, book and book's, books and books'. If you cannot decide which spelling to use, you need only remember how to indicate ownership. That is to say, you must learn how to indicate the possession of something.

Their and *theirs* are used to indicate that something belongs to a person or thing. *There* is used with a verb. Remember: there is, there are, there was, there were – t h e r e spells there. This spelling is also used for a place. Is anyone there? There is their house, over there.

My, his, her, *its*, our, your and *their* are possessive adjectives: my book, her eyes, its leaves, and their house. Mine, his, hers, *its*, ours yours and *theirs* are possessive pronouns. This book is mine; this is yours; and these are *theirs*. Remember this rule: e in her, i in his, e and i in their.

It's means it is, just as can't means cannot, don't means do not, that's means that is, they're means they are, and won't means will not. However, unless you are writing to a friend, or reporting a conversation in quotation marks, it is best to avoid such contractions (see colloquial English, p. 68).

An s is added to many nouns (names of things, see table 27) to make them plural: book becomes books; but man becomes men. To indicate ownership either an apostrophe (') or an apostrophe s ('s) is added to a word (book's and men's) or just an apostrophe is added (books'). For example: the cat's dinner (the dinner of the cat); the cats' dinner (the dinner of the cats); the man's books (the books of the man); the men's books (the books of the men); the books' covers (the covers of the books); the book's cover (the cover of the book); Thomas's pen (the pen of Thomas); and St James's Church (the Church of St James).

Improve your writing

1 *Exercises in dictation*, with first seen and then unseen passages, provide practice in both punctuation and spelling; and help you to increase your writing speed. You also learn about your subject if exercises in dictation are given by teachers of other subjects as well as by teachers of English.

When teachers dictate notes, they should check that important words are spelt correctly, either by marking the work or by writing these words on the blackboard at the end of the dictation so that the students can check their own work.

2 Make a note, from your dictionary, of the correct spelling of any word marked by a teacher so that you can learn it. It is a good idea to keep an indexed notebook for this purpose so that you can try not to spell any word incorrectly more than once.

3 *Spelling test.* Ask someone to test your spelling of these words:

absence, accelerate, accidentally, accommodate, achieved, acquaint, address, altogether, already, ancillary, apparent, attendance, audience, auxiliary,
beauty, beginning, bureaucracy,
calendar, cereal, competence, conscience, conscientious, consensus,
definite, desperate, develop, disappear, disappoint,
embarrass, emperor, exaggerate, existence,
fascinate, forty, fourth, fulfil, fulfilled,
gauge,
harmful, hierarchy, humorous
incidentally, independent,
liaison,
misspell,
necessary, noticeably,
occasion, occurred, omit, omitted,
parallel, personnel, possess, precede, privilege, procedure, proceed, pursued,

receive, recommend, relevant, rhythm,
scissors, seize, separate, severely, siege, successful, syllable,
unnecessarily, until,
wholly,
yield.

4 Take an interest in the study of the origins of words (etymology).
This will help you to understand why some words are spelt in a
particular way. For example, the word separate is derived from a
Latin word *separare* (to separate or divide); so is another English
word, pare, meaning to cut one's nails or to peel (potatoes, for
example).

5 Do not get into the habit of using another word when you are not
sure of the spelling of the most appropriate word. Instead, always
refer to a dictionary so that you can use the word that best conveys
your meaning.

Appendix 3

The use of numbers in writing

Except in scientific writing, numbers less than 100 are usually written in words: and symbols should be avoided. The number of the year should always be written in figures, and dates should be written *either* 20 January 1995, *or* 20th January 1995. Roman numerals may be used for the names of monarchs: Queen Elizabeth II *or* Queen Elizabeth the Second.

In writing, cardinal numbers (twenty-one to ninety-nine) and ordinal numbers (e.g. twenty-first, one-hundred-and-first) should be hyphenated.

Always use words, not figures, at the beginning of a sentence, and for numbers one to nine, even in scientific writing. Note also that two numbers should not be written together either as numerals or words, because ambiguity may result: write two 50 W lamps, not 2 50 W nor two fifty watt.

Decimals are indicated by a full stop on the line or, in some countries, by a comma. In scientific writing the comma should not, therefore, be used to break numbers above 999 into groups of three digits. With more than four digits, spaces should be left: 9999 or 10 000 or 999 999, etc. Because of differences between European and USA usage, the words billion, trillion and quadrillion should not be used.

Most countries have adopted the metric system of measurement and use the International System of Units (SI units: see table 28). If it is necessary to use symbols, instead of words, the following rules apply. Leave a space between the number and the symbol (50 W and 20 °C). Do not put a full stop after the symbol unless this comes at the end of a sentence. And do not add an s to any symbol to make it plural (m = metre and metres).

Table 28   *International System of Units (SI units)*

Quantity	Unit	Symbol
length	millimetre (0. 001 m)	mm
	centimetre (0.01 m)	cm
	metre	m
	kilometre (1000 m)	km
area	square centimetre	cm²
	square metre	m²
	hectare	ha
volume	cubic centimetre	cm³
	cubic metre	m³
capacity	millilitre (0.001 l)	ml
	litre	l
mass	gramme (0.001 kg)	g
	kilogramme	kg
	tonne (1000 kg)	t
density	kilogramme per cubic metre	kg/m³
time	second	s
	minute (60 s)	min
	hour (3600 s)	h
	day (86 400 s)	d
speed, velocity	metre per second	m/s
	kilometre per second	km/s
temperature (*t*)	degree Celsius	C

Notes. The International System of Units includes *base units* (e.g. the metre, kilogramme and second); and *derived units* (e.g. centimetre and gramme). The litre, tonne, minute, hour, day and degree Celsius are recognized units outside the International System. The hectare is accepted temporarily in view of existing practice. In Britain the degree Celsius used to be called the degree Centigrade. For further information on SI units, including units not shown in this table, see the *British Standard* BS 5555 or the identical *International Standard* ISO 1000.

Appendix 4
Further reading

Dictionaries

A good dictionary gives the spelling, pronunciation and meaning of each word, its use in current English, its derivatives (words formed from it), and its derivation. Make sure that your dictionary gives all this information. Suitable dictionaries for students include *Chambers' Twentieth Century Dictionary* (Chambers, Edinburgh), *Collins Dictionary of the English Language* (Collins, London), *The Concise Oxford Dictionary* (Oxford University Press, Oxford), and *Webster's New Collegiate Dictionary* (Merriam, Mass.).

Reference books

Flesch, R. F. (1962), *The Art of Plain Talk*, London and New York, Collier-Macmillan.

Fowler, H. W. (1968), *Dictionary of Modern English Usage*, 2nd edn. rev. Sir Ernest Gowers, London, Oxford University Press.

Gowers, E. (1973), *The Complete Plain Words*, 2nd edn. rev. Sir Bruce Fraser, London, HMSO.

Napley, D. (1975), *The Technique of Persuasion*, 2nd edn, London, Sweet & Maxwell.

Partridge, E. (1965), *Usage and Abusage: A Guide to Good English*, 8th edn, London and New York, Hamish Hamilton and British Book Centre.

Perrin, P. G. (1965), *Writer's Guide and Index to English*, 4th edn rev. K. W. Dickens and W. R. Ebbitt, Fair Lawn, N.J., Scott, Foresman & Co.

Vallins, G. H. (1964), *Good English: How to Write It*, London and Washington, André Deutsch and Academic Press.

Index

abbreviations, 31, 63–4, 94
accuracy: in writing, 3, 15, 31, 63, 77,
    87; of citations, 100, 108; of
    diagrams, 34, 35; of quotations, 134;
    of records, 25, 32
acknowledgements, 105, 108
acronyms, 64
address: in letters, 19–21, 27; on
    envelope, 23, 25
adjective, 130, 133, 138
adverb, 120
ambiguity, 3, 47, 51, 67–8, 77, 114
answers, see questions
apostrophe, 133, 138
appendices, 76, 105
applications, 25–9, 121
appropriateness, 25, 31, 42, 47, 58, 81
argument, 5, 31, 43, 47, 49, 80
arrangement, 31, 44, 104–6; see also
    headings, order, topic outline
asides, 83, 133
assessment, 1–6, 103–4; see also
    marking answers
assignments, see course work, essays,
    extended essays, questions
assumptions, 80

balance, 31, 45, 51, 84

beginning, 44, 81, 83; see also
    introduction
bias, 15, 31, 47, 91
bibliographic details, 100, 108
bibliography, see references
books, 95–7, 112, 143
brackets (parentheses), 133
brevity, 46, 54, 77; see also conciseness,
    simplicity

capital letters, 131
care, 30, 50–1, 67, 112
checking: composition, 47–9, 51–2;
    extended essay, 108–9; lecture
    notes, 11; project report, 108–9
circumlocution, 69–77
citation, 108
clarity, 1–5, 7, 17, 30, 31, 32, 48, 54, 77,
    88, 113, 129, 133, 134
clichés, 54, 69, 75, 114
coherence, see unity
colon, 133
comma, 84, 131–3
comment words, 77, 87
communication, 2, 4, 8, 16, 46, 47; aids
    to, 62, 129; barriers to, 47, 48, 62, 73,
    135
communications, 17, 30, 41–52

146   *Students Must Write*

completeness, 1, 3, 30, 31, 51, 63, 66, 113
composition, 3, 32, 41–52
comprehension, 1, 2, 65–6
conciseness, 2, 17, 30, 48, 77, 82
conclusion, 43, 46, 49, 83, 105
conclusions, 80
conjecture, 80
conjunction, 130, 132
connections (links), 44, 45, 46, 67, 77, 80, 81, 87, 130
consistency, 31
context, 67, 81
control, 31, 43, 81, 83
copies (as a record), 29, 110
copying, 12, 98, 108
correspondence, 16–29
course work, 1, 6, 30, 43, 52, 63, 65, 66, 68, 81, 100, 103; common faults in, 50–1; *see also* exercises
courtesy, 17, 31
creativity, 49
criticism: of others, 38–40, 47, 50; of own work, 47–9, 51–2
curriculum vitae, 26, 28

dash, 84, 133
data, 12, 32
date, 24, 141
decimals, 141
definitions, 43, 62, 63, 65
derivation, 143
derivatives, 143
description, 12–13, 14
details, 42, 43
diagrams, 32–7, 43, 83, 106
diary, 6, 12, 88–9
dictionary, 53, 57, 63, 67, 135, 143
digression, 43, 46
directness, 49; *see also* simplicity
directories, 95
discussion, 117; in report, 105, 108; *see also* exercises, talking, tutorials
documentation, *see* references
double negatives, 75
draft, 47, 48, 109
drawings, 12, 32

elegant variation, 67
emphasis, 17, 43, 46, 67, 81, 83–5, 131
enclosures, 19, 21, 26, 27
encyclopaedias, 94–5
ending, 44, 46, 83; *see also* conclusion
English: business, 18; good, 31; plain, 54, 142; poor, 2–3, 5; slang, 68; standard, 68; teaching, 4–5, 14; use of, 4–5
essay writing, 1, 42–52
etymology, 140, 143
euphony, 85, 86
evidence, 31, 44, 47, 49, 80, 113
examination: performance, 6, 100; preparing for, 1, 10, 63, 66, 97, 98, 111–14; technique, 1–3, 43, 52, 68, 81, 114–18
examiners, 1, 112–14, 115, 116; reports of, 1–3, 112–14
examples, 42, 44, 47, 113, 133
exclamation mark, 131
exercises: allocating your time, 6; answering questions, 119; checking, 108–9; comprehension, 65–6, 78; criticism, 15, 50–2; definition, 65; description, 15; dictation, 139; discussion, 6, 15, 50, 114; editing, 87; essay writing, 50; instructions, 40; letter writing, 25; making notes, 14, 100; meaning of words, 64–6, 140; précis, 77–9; punctuation, 134, 139; reading, 6, 52, 87–92; speaking, 124; spelling, 139; studying, 100, 118; summary, 78–9; topic outline, 50, 65, 119
explanation, 30, 31, 32, 62, 75, 133
exposition, 49
extended essay, 102–10

facts, 59, 80
figure of speech, 75, 78
figures, *see* illustrations
first draft, 47, 48, 109
first person, 75
footnotes, 82
forceful language, 5, 44, 49, 76, 84

foreign words, 64, 75, 84
full stop, 131, 133, 141, 142

gathering information and ideas, 41, 93, 94
grammar, 2, 3, 5, 87, 114
graphs, 32, 34

hackneyed phrases, *see* clichés
handbooks, 95, 143
handwriting, 5, 11, 29, 113, 118, 131, 139
headings: in composition, 42, 80, 81, 83; in extended essay, 105–6; in notes, 9; in project report, 105–6; of illustrations, 32; of instructions, 30; of letter, 19, 24; of table, 82
histogram, 34, 35

ideas, 12, 42, 44
idiom, 69, 94
illustrations, 32–7, 107–8
imagination, 30
impartiality, 31
information: conveying, 42–52, 108; finding, 43, 93–100; sources, 108; storing, 100
instructions, 30; preparing, 5, 16, 30–1, 40
interest, 7, 30, 44, 47, 51, 77, 81, 86, 87, 90
International System of Units (SI units), 141, 142
interviews, 25, 120–3
introduction, 42, 43, 81, 83
inverted commas (quotation marks), 57, 134
italic print, 84
it is (it's) and its, 138

jargon, 70, 75, 76
journals, 97

knowledge, 3, 99, 113, 117

language: appropriate, 25, 31, 42, 47, 58, 81; colloquial, 68, 114, 133, 138;

correct use of, 4–5; idiomatic, 69, 94; of your subject, 56, 62–3; slang, 68; standard, 68
learning, 3, 4, 12, 49, 50, 62, 78, 89, 99, 111, 118
lecture notes, 8–12, 14
lecturing, 9–10; *see also* talking
letter writing, 17–29, 43
library, use of, 94–7
links, *see* connections
logical arrangement, 31, 44, 47, 80

manuals (handbooks), 95, 143
marking answers, 51, 52, 112–15
marks (for answers), 1, 114–15
meaning: conveying, 44, 45, 47, 51, 75, 77, 134; of abbreviations, 63–4, 94; of questions, 2, 51, 65; *see also* words
measurement, 31, 34, 82, 141
metaphor, 75
momentum, 43, 81, 87

names, 31, 84, 129
narration, 13
notes: for guidance, 106; from reading, 98–100; of ideas, 12; of lectures, 8–12, 14; of practical work, 12; storing, 10, 100; use of, 1, 12, 99
noun, 70, 130
numbering, 109; illustrations, 32, 109; instructions, 31; items in list, 84; pages of report, 110; tables, 82, 109
numbers, use of, 31, 37, 141–2

observation, 13, 51; aids to, 8, 32; record of, 12, 15, 32–3
only (word out of place), 67–8
opinion, 80
order, 2, 13, 17, 30, 42, 43–6, 47, 81, 113
organization, *see* planning
originality, 49, 93, 103
outline, *see* topic outline
ownership (how to indicate), 138–9

padding, 76

page numbers, 110
paragraphs, 42–6, 47, 86; break
    between, 44, 74; length of, 46, 83, 91
parenthesis (brackets), 84, 133
parts of report, 104–6
parts of speech, 130
period (full stop), 131, 133, 141, 142
periodicals, 97
persuasiveness, 31, 49, 91, 143
phrases: hackneyed, *see* cliches,
    superfluous, 44–5, 83
planning: compositions, 3, 14, 41–6,
    50–1, 86, 105; studies, 6, 100, 111–12,
    118; *see also* questions, topic outline
plural, 64, 133, 138, 142
pomposity, 56
possessive, 133, 138–9
postcard, 22
practical work, 12
précis, 1, 177–9
precision, 31, 37, 45, 51, 54, 57, 59, 63,
    69, 77, 87
prejudice, *see* bias
preparation, 9, 14, 32, 41–3, 124–6; *see*
    also examinations, report
preposition, 58, 130
presentation, 31; of letter, 17, 25, 29; of
    report, 104–6, 110
project report, 102–10
pronoun, 130, 133, 138
pronunciation, 135, 143
punctuation, 2, 3, 5, 31, 44, 74, 85,
    114, 129–34; of abbreviations, 64,
    142; of numbers, 140
purpose: of reader, 98; of writer, 31,
    41, 42, 43, 44, 49, 51, 70, 81, 102

question mark, 131
questions: answering, 1–4, 41–52, 63,
    65, 66, 81, 112–18, 119; asking, 9, 10,
    14, 120, 123, 124; in course work,
    50–2; in examinations, 2–3, 112–18,
    119; of reader, 41–2, 81, 86, 105; *see*
    also discussion, interview
quotation marks (inverted commas),
    57, 134

quotations, 108, 134

reader: consideration for, 17, 24, 31,
    41, 47, 62, 86; effect on, 5, 26, 29, 31,
    32, 34–5, 37, 44, 46, 47, 49, 70, 84,
    86; helping, 32, 34, 42, 44, 46, 49, 53,
    54, 77, 80–92, 132; needs of, 41–2,
    43, 48, 49, 74, 80, 85, 91, 106
reading, 51, 136; before lectures, 9, 10;
    good English, 6, 87–92; how to
    read, 3, 98–100; questions, 3, 65,
    112–13, 115, 116; what to read, 52,
    88–92; *see also* information, finding
records, 8–13, 25, 32–3; *see also* notes
reference: books, 94–5, 243; terms of,
    103
references: bibliographic, 100; cards
    for, 99–100; list of, 100, 108; to
    illustrations and tables, 108
relevance, 1, 3, 31, 43, 44, 81, 84
remembering, 8, 10, 12
repetition, 42, 43, 46, 74, 108; of
    sound, 85; of words, 67, 84; *see also*
    tautology
report: of examiners, 1–3, 112–14; of
    project, 102–10; preparing, 12, 43,
    76, 102–10; sections of, 105–6
revision: for examination, 10, 98, 99,
    111–12, 118; of composition, 7, 41,
    47–9, 74; of notes, 10, 11, 99
rhythm, 85

scope (of composition), 41, 42, 44, 81,
    102
selection, 42–3, 49
self-expression, 3, 4–5, 13, 15, 16, 49,
    75; *see also* ambiguity, originality
self-improvement, 2, 5, 38; *see also*
    exercises
semi-colon, 133, 134
seminars, 124
sentence, 67, 81, 86, 129–30;
    arrangement, 44; construction, 70,
    83; length of, 84–5, 91, 131; purpose
    of, 43, 44; simple, 132
signposts (for reader), 42, 44, 134

simile, 75
simplicity, 1, 6, 17, 30, 32, 43, 48, 62, 65, 77, 88
sincerity, 32, 86
slang, 114
sources of information, 93–100, 108
speaking, *see* talking
speaking and writing, 48, 68, 83, 87; differences, 9, 74
speculation, 46
speech, parts of, 130
spelling, 2, 3, 4, 31, 47, 63, 143
study, 6, 10–12, 14, 78, 88, 99, 100, 111–12, 118–19
style, 74, 80, 85–6, 89, 90, 91
summary, 1, 46, 77–9, 105
supervision, 102, 103, 106, 108, 109
syllable, 136
syllabus, 8, 106
symbols, 36, 82, 141–2

talking, 120–8
tautology, 60
teaching: of English, 4–5; purpose of, 3–4; *see also* exercises
technical writing, 56
terms: of reference, 103; technical, 56, 62–3, 94
their and there, 138
thinking, 4, 16, 69; about questions, 2, 3, 65, 112–13, 115, 116; and writing, 7, 8, 13–14, 41, 52, 74, 77; in lectures, 9; memoranda, 12; whilst reading, 3, 98; with words, 53, 114
thoroughness, 46; *see also* completeness
time, allocation of, 6, 12, 91, 93, 95, 100, 102, 106, 107, 111, 112, 115–16
timetable, 6, 111, 118
timing, 31
title, 9, 80, 83, 84, 134
tone of letters, 18, 24
topic: of paragraph, 42, 43, 44; outline, 9, 12, 42–3, 44, 47, 65, 81, 93, 99,

113, 119; sentence, 44
tutorials, 123–4

underlining, 43, 84, 134
understanding: demonstrating, 1, 44, 62, 113; your work, 4, 9, 14, 48, 49, 63, 65, 66, 99, 118
units, 32, 34, 82, 140–1
unity (coherence), 32, 43, 44, 46, 47, 77

verb, 70, 130
verbosity, reasons for, 73; *see also* words, too many
visual aids, 125, 127–8
vocabulary, 53, 54, 62, 65, 80, 91, 114, 136
voice, active and passive, 70, 75–6

wholeness, *see* unity
words: arranging, 44; choice of, 43, 47, 54, 63, 67–79, 140; intensifying, 37; length of, 51, 54–6, 75, 91; meaning of, 54, 57–63, 65–6, 73, 77, 142; misuse of, 47–8, 57–61; modifying, 37; number of, 47, 69–77, 117; of subject, 56, 62–3, 94; origins of, 140, 143; plain, 54, 143; position of, 67–8, 85; qualifying, 59, 61; repetition of, 67, 84; sounds of, 85; superfluous, 44, 47, 69–77, 83; too few, 47, 70; too many, 47, 69–77, 83; unimportant, 44; use of, 47, 63, 67–79, 90; used in questions, 65
writing, 49; and learning, 49; and reading, 91; and speaking, 9, 48, 68, 74, 83, 87; and thinking, 3, 13–14; approach to, 31; common faults in, 6, 50–1, 112–14; imaginative, 30; importance of, 1, 5; kinds of, 13, 30; materials for, 10, 25, 100–1; pleasure from, 48–9, 53; poor, 2–3, 5, 49; practice, 6; reasons for, 8; rules for, 49; teaching of, 2, 4, 15; *see also* composition, exercises, handwriting